Residential

DEFEND THE ASSETS!

"Residential Care Fees
Defend The Assets!"
supersedes
"Residential Care Fees:
Don't Let Them Grab The House!"
which was first published in March 1996 and
ran to numerous revised reprints.

Residential Care Fees

DEFEND THE ASSETS!

By William Neilson, MA.,LLB.
Advocate

with a contribution by a
Member of the Chartered Institute of Taxation

SPINNING ACORN
EDINBURGH

Published in Scotland by
Spinning Acorn,
Edinburgh.

First published February 1999
Reprinted with amendments February 2000

Copyright
The author 2000

Set in ITC Officina
and Times New Roman

Printed by Anthony Rowe Limited,
Chippenham, Wiltshire.

ISBN 0 9522762 5 9

British Library Cataloguing-in-Publication Data
A catalogue record for this book is available
from the British Library

All rights reserved. No part of this publication may be
reproduced, stored in a retrieval system, or transmitted,
in any form or by any means, electronic, mechanical,
photocopying, recording, or otherwise without the
prior permission of the publishers.

"Spinning Acorn" is an imprint belonging to Spinning Acorn Ltd,
Registered in Scotland, Registration Number 169128,
Registered Office: (214), 44 Morningside Road, Edinburgh, EH10 4 BF.
VAT registration 671 2274 44.

Contents

Preface		7
Ch 1	Know The Rules	9
Ch 2	Dispose of the Assets	24
Ch 3	Postpone the Day	34
Ch 4	Defend a Deprivation	39
Ch 5	Avoid Insolvency Proceedings	57
Ch 6	Render Unto Caesar	62
Summary of Time Limits and Escape Routes		69
Draft Discretionary Trust Deed		71
The Legislation		75
Yule v South Lanarkshire Council (No 2)		92
Index		95

PUBLISHERS NOTICE

The authors and publishers accept no liability for any of the consequences which may arise from reliance on the commentary contained in this book. While we believe it provides a legally unassailable solution no-one can forecast the interpretation which may be applied by the courts; nor can a book issued to the public at large take account of individual circumstances in the way that a professional adviser, in direct contact with his client, can. We therefore recommend that professional advice should be sought in all cases.

SPINNING ACORN

Preface

When *Residential Care Fees: Don't Let Them Grab The House!* was first published in March 1996 solicitors were under siege from elderly clients and their relatives, all afraid that the family inheritance would be seized to pay for care, and demanding advice on how to put assets beyond the reach of the local authority. Despite a change of government, and in the face of recommendations from a Royal Commission, the law remains unaltered, and is likely to remain so for some time. The elderly are, with justification, still worried about losing the house and other assets to pay for long term care.

To assist them and their advisers this latest version of the book sets out the rules and shows the best way to dispose of assets to protect them from inclusion in a care fees assessment using a device which provides not only greater security for the elderly person but also a stouter defence against the local authority. There is however a new problem to be faced. Local authorities are increasingly challenging earlier disposals made by elderly persons who are now in care and, depending on when a disposal was carried out, are seeking to have the transaction rescinded, or are calculating the assessment as though the disposal had never taken place.

To help meet this challenge lengthy new sections have been added on ways of either avoiding a confrontation with the local authority or defending a disposal if they mount an attack. Reassurance is given to the elderly person who is in care, wondering perhaps, as the legal arguments proceed, whether he can be put out on the street, and also to relatives to whom property may have been gifted who may now think themselves vulnerable to a retrieval exercise by the local authority.

The Royal Commission on Funding of Long Term Care for the Elderly

A recommendation by the Royal Commission (which reported on 1st March 1999) that elderly persons should have to pay only for the residential part of their care and that "personal" (comparable to "nursing" or "therapeutic") services, where required, will be paid for by the state (as they are in hospital) was widely welcomed by all those who have campaigned for such a logical solution. Nevertheless many elderly persons would still face the prospect of savings being used up to pay for

Preface

residential care on its own, and the Commission has recommended that this basic element of care, which can be a substantial burden, continue to be funded on a means-tested basis out of income and savings (not excluding the house).

Unfortunately the Commission's proposals, however modest, were merely noted "with interest" by the Government and are unlikely to be implemented in the near future. While the limits on resources which cannot be taken into account in a care fees assessment (see **1.17**) could be quickly raised by amending regulations, a fundamental change like that recommended by the Royal Commission would require primary legislation. A government which has already proved itself long on promises but short on delivery may not be too eager to increase the welfare budget by the billion pounds which implementation of the Commission's proposals could require. Nothing was included in the Queen's Speech to the Westminster parliament in November 1999, and there is no sign in the current Scottish legislative programme of a desire to set up separate rules, and funding, for long term care in Scotland. There will therefore be no substantial change to the primary legislation for a year or more, if even then. The most that may be hoped for is that the problem will once again become the subject of an election "promise", although this means that nothing will be done until after the next election, and with a new government thereafter safely in power, as little may be done then as has been done to date.

1

Know
The Rules

If assets are to be safely disposed of to avoid their inclusion in a residential care fees assessment, or if such a disposal is later challenged by a local authority after the entry to care, it is essential to know in detail the rules which govern the local authorities' powers and duties as the information provided by some local authorities, whether due to mistake or guile, may be less than accurate.

Assessment Procedures

1.2 The current assessment procedures are as follows: when it comes to the attention of a local authority that a person, usually elderly, in their area may require residential care they have first to carry out an assessment of **need** under **section 47** of the **National Health Service and Community Care Act 1990** (in **England and Wales**) or **section 12A** of the **Social Work (Scotland) Act 1968** (in **Scotland**). If they conclude that a place in a residential home is required, they take legal responsibility for paying the fees at a **"standard rate"** (as defined in **section 22(2)** of the **National Assistance Act 1948**) for what is known as **Part III accommodation.** This is accommodation either provided by the local authority or the provision of which is secured from other bodies by the local authority (**section 21(8)** of the **Health and Social Services and Social Security Adjudications Act 1983).** (In **Scotland** this is sometimes referred to as **"Part IV"** accommodation because the providing and securing provisions are found in **Part IV** of the **1968 Act**).

1.3 Although it is the local authority who have the legal responsibility for paying the basic fees they are also empowered, and required, to carry out a second, **means**, assessment of the resident and make him contribute to these fees out of his income and, if that is insufficient, out of his capital too. This is a matter of law laid down in the **1948 Act** at **sections 22** and **26**, as amended by the **National Assistance (Assessment of Resources) Regulations 1992 (S.I. No. 2997).** Sections 22 and 26 of the **1948 Act** as amended by **section 87** of the **Social Work (Scotland) Act 1968** apply also to **Scotland**. The **National Assistance (Sums for Personal Requirements) Regulations** which are revised annually allow the resident to retain a small sum (currently £14.75 per week by virtue of **S.I. 1999 No 549**) for personal expenses.

Know the Rules

1.4 Further powers allow the local authority to lay claim to the assets of those who do not comply **(see 1.9 (i))**, or to recover their value (as at the date of transfer, and limited to the extent of the fees debt at the date the request is made) from those to whom they have been donated or transferred in exchange for a sum which is less than their market value **(see 1.15)**. However if the local authority are unsuccessful in recovering the fees from the resident's assets, or those to whom he has transferred them, they cannot simply stop providing, or paying for, the resident's care. Even if there is a dispute over the local authority's claim and in the meantime a fees debt mounts up the local authority must continue to provide the care or pay the fees. The local authority's obligations persist even in the face of a failure by them to recover the expenditure from the resident or other party. The resident cannot be evicted from care on grounds of non-payment.

1.5 Most local authorities fulfil their obligations to those who are assessed as being in need of care by means of contracts with residential home owners but the resident can choose a place outwith these arrangements if it will not cost the local authority more. Any elderly person who can afford it can of course bypass the local authority and make his own arrangements with a care home and thereby avoid all local bureaucratic involvement. See **2.3** to **2.7** for details of how this choice can be made more feasible if **attendance allowance** is payable by the Department of Social Security.

1.6 The **National Health Service and Community Care Act 1990** came into force on **1st April 1993**. Its introduction was supposed to improve standards of care, but its true effect was to shift financial responsibility for the elderly from central government to short-of-cash local authorities. Under the new arrangements instead of the Department of Social Security assessing a person's assets and needs and paying income support towards the cost of residential care, local authorities now have to do the assessment and, subject to none-too-generous limits, extract the cost of care from the resident's assets insofar as his pension and other income falls short. Thus a system of national uniformity in its application has been replaced by one which varies in practice from one local authority to another, and, as with the old parish poor law, the poorest areas which generate least income, but have the greatest need, are worst served.

However if a resident is poor enough to qualify for **income support** prior to entry to care it may continue to be paid, and eligibility may improve after entry to care as at that point the disqualifying level of savings rises from £8,000 to £16,000 - see regulations 45 and 53 of the Income Support (General) Regulations 1987 (S.I.No 1967) as amended by regulation 12 of the Income-related Benefits Schemes (Miscellaneous Amendments) Regulations 1996 (S.I. No 4620). Deprivation rules apply here too: a claimant who gives away property with the intention of qualifying himself for income support will receive nothing but a polite refusal.

Beware The Difference

1.7 As the regulations under which the local authorities now operate are closely modelled on, or simply refer to, the social security income support regulations, decisions of the courts or Social Security Commissioners on these regulations can provide a useful guide to how the local authority regulations will be interpreted, but when a problem arises it is necessary to look closely at the relevant regulations: sometimes the rules which are to be applied by the local authorities in making a **means assessment** for residential care purposes are not exactly the same as those which are to be applied by the Department of Social Security in assessing **eligibility** for income support.

1.8 For example if the DSS discover **notional capital (see 1.14)** they simply do not pay income support or reduce the amount payable, possession in their case really being nine-tenths of the law. If the department's decision is upheld by a Social Security Appeal Tribunal or Commissioner the DSS owe nobody anything. The local authority on the other hand are something of a pig in the middle as they must continue to pay the residential care fees and can use a discovery of notional capital only to increase the contribution which the resident is **assessed** as being bound to make. The withholding remedy available to the DSS is not available to the local authority. Actual recovery of the money from the resident or those to whom he has disposed of assets is a rather more difficult process **(Ch 4).**

1.9 The following are examples of the differences:

(i) the local authority (by virtue of **section 22 (for England and Wales)** and **section 23 (for Scotland)** of the **Health and Social Services and Social Security Adjudications Act 1983)** have power to create a legal charge over any land (i.e. any real or heritable property, not just the house) in which the resident has a proprietorial interest whereby they can eventually claim on the sale proceeds for what is owed to them for the fees (which they are bound to pay the care provider) while the DSS do not have, or need, a similar power with regard to payment of income support.

(ii) where the resident's house is put up for sale the DSS will disregard its value for six months, or longer in some cases, in assessing eligibility for income support whereas the local authority must, regardless of any intention to sell, take the value of the house into account immediately in making the assessment of means which decides how much the resident has to pay for care.

(iii) the local authority have discretionary power to ignore the capital value of the house where it continues to be occupied by a relative who does not otherwise qualify, or a non-relative who has had a special relationship with an owner who vacates it to go into care (**paragraph 18** of **Schedule 4** to the

National Assistance (Assessment of Resources) Regulations 1992 (S.I. No. 2977) - see 1.23-1.24.1). The DSS do not have similar discretionary power in deciding eligibility for income support.

1.10 A further notable difference of a **procedural** nature lies in the well established DSS administrative **appeals system** whereby the department's decision, on income support for example, can be appealed to a Social Security Appeal Tribunal and to a Social Security Commissioner with the claimant usually represented by a layman such as a welfare rights officer. Commissioners' decisions provide legal precedents for the department and Tribunals. A challenge to a local authority assessment on the other hand has to use the **complaints procedure** established under section 7B of the Local Authority Social Services Act 1970 (in England and Wales) or section 5A of the Social Work (Scotland) Act 1968 (these provisions having been inserted by sections 50 and 52 respectively of the National Health and Community Care Act 1990). Unlike the social security system this procedure will yield no legal precedents, but with both systems there is of course an alternative, or eventual, resort to the courts available **(see 4.10)**. (And where a case concerns a local authority's legal obligations judicial review rather than the complaints procedure must be used - *R v Gloucestershire CC, ex p Radar* (1998) 1 C.C.L. Rep 476.)

1.11 It is important to bear these and other differences in mind and to realise that the local authority rules are a different legal code where the precedents and practices of the DSS with regard to the distribution of income support could sometimes be helpful and at other times misleading.

Note: Social Security Commissioners' decisions which are binding on Social Security Tribunals and the department can be consulted at the Commissioners' offices at 23 Melville Street, Edinburgh and 83 Farringdon Street, London or obtained on subscription. Decisions are initially given a "C" reference e.g. CIS/999/97 and many progress no further. Some which have been circulated among the other Commissioners because the Commissioner who made the decision thinks it raises points of general importance are given a star e.g. *33/96. If a decision is deemed by the Chief Commissioner as worthy of being "reported" it will be given a new "R" reference and can be bought from the Stationery Office or inspected at local DSS offices. Such a decision is then binding on other Commissioners unless overturned by a Tribunal of Commissioners whose decisions are promulgated in a similar manner.

Capital Assessment

1.12 The local authority will take the resident's **capital and income** into account in deciding how much he has to pay towards residential care they provide or care fees they incur on his behalf. **Capital** in this context includes money, shares and property which belong to the resident but excludes any asset which he has transferred to another party provided the transfer has been carried out with no demonstrable intention of avoiding a liability to pay care fees (**see 2.20-2.23**). Capital for these purposes comes in two forms, actual, and notional.

Actual Capital

1.13   **Actual** capital obviously includes the house, cash in hand, or under the bed, savings in a bank, etc. Less obviously, it also includes assets which are not in person's possession but to which he has a right which is not immediately realisable, and can include for example a payout under a will which will not be received until the estate is wound up, or an interest in certain trusts. If such capital is treated as actual capital for assessment purposes it will be a drain on the resident's resources because, as far as the resident is concerned, it remains "notional" until he actually receives it. Where, for example, money is due out of an executry it can be argued that it should not be treated as actual capital until the executors have had sufficient time to wind up the estate, which will vary with its complexity.

Notional Capital

1.14   **Notional** capital on the other hand includes capital which one has given away in certain circumstances or to which one could lay immediate claim. **Regulation 25** of the **National Assistance (Assessment of Resources) Regulations 1992 (S.I. No. 2977)** allows the local authority, at their discretion, to treat a resident as **notionally** possessing capital of which he has, **at any time in the past**, deprived himself for the purpose of decreasing the amount he may be liable to pay for his residential care but they have to be able to satisfy themselves that the avoidance of liability for fees was a **significant** factor in the decision to dispose of assets. A reference in **Regulation 25(2)** to the Income Support General Regulations 1987 (S.I. No 1967) means that "deprivation of capital" also includes not claiming funds to which one has a right, the unredeemed prize winning lottery ticket being an obvious example, (although of course if the proceeds were large enough there would be no need to bother the local authority further about residential care).

1.15   It should be noted however that nothing in **these regulations themselves** gives the local authority power to seize the resident's assets if they have been transferred, even if it can be proved that they were transferred with a view to avoiding liability for fees. Their only specific power to nullify the effect of such transactions by reclaiming their value (to the extent of the fees debt) from the person or body to whom they were transferred, lies in **section 21** of the **Health and Social Services and Social Security Adjudications Act 1983.** That provision affects only transactions where **nothing was paid** or the payment was **less than the market value** of the asset **and** the transaction took place within the **six months** prior to entry to, or while residing in, **Part III accommodation. None of these factors is conclusive however. It is the donor's intention at the date of donation which rules the matter. If an** intention to avoid liability for care fees cannot be proved (or an allegation to that effect can be rebutted) section 21 cannot be applied to the transferees no matter how close the date of transfer is to the date of entry to care (see section 21(1)(b)).

Tariff Income

1.16   If the total value of all capital assets **(actual or notional - see regulation 25(5) of the 1992 Regulations)** is less than £10,000 it is disregarded. Where its value is between £10,000 and £16,000 it is assumed to provide a weekly income (known as **"tariff income"**) of £1 for every £250 or part of £250 over £10,000 (**Regulation 28** of the **1992 Regulations**). Therefore a resident with £16,000 is treated as having an imaginary weekly income of £24 from his capital which is far in excess of what it can earn even if it is actual and all in cash in a high income account (these notional rates having been first set years ago when interest rates were high and remaining unchanged as rates fell). Residents with this range of capital actually in their possession or attributed to them (whose real income falls short of the care fees) have to pay between £1 and £24 per week towards the fees, this being in effect a levy on their capital which will rapidly deplete their already meagre assets. (The artificiality of the process is amply demonstrated by **Regulation 22(4)** which provides for any **actual income**, which this rapidly diminishing capital continues to produce, to be treated as **capital**). What is really achieved is a highly stepped transition from being assessed as due to pay nothing out of capital (if £10,000 or less) to paying the whole care fee (if capital £16,000 or more).

1.17   Where the capital itself is notional **Regulation 26(2)** of the **1992 Regulations** does however allow this reduction in capital by assessment of an imaginary income to be recognised so that the **notional** capital is regarded as diminished on the basis of the difference between a fees contribution assessed to reflect it and one which ignores it. No such rule is required for **actual** capital as the effect of the levy is all too obvious where, for example, a savings account will be diminished every week by amounts far in excess of anything it would ever earn. Residents with over £16,000 in capital have to pay the whole weekly fee regardless of the income it actually produces, and irrespective of the amount of income, however small, from other sources such as pensions. The increase in the capital limits (since **8th April 1996**) from £3,000 to £10,000 and from £8,000 to £16,000 by **regulations 20** and **28** of the **National Assistance (Assessment of Resources) Regulations 1992 (S.I. No. 2977)** as amended has therefore only slightly alleviated the problem faced by elderly persons possessed of assets, whose income is too low to cover the care fees.

Capital Exhaustion

1.18   It is sometimes wrongly assumed that the capital of £10,000 or less which should be disregarded in the means assessment becomes in some way immune from **debt recovery procedures** which a local authority (or indeed any other creditor) may apply. While often enough the person with less than £10,000 capital will never owe the local authority anything, if he has income he will be assessed as due to hand that over as a contribution to his care fees. If he fails to hand it over, and thereby runs up a debt to the local authority, the capital of whatever amount can, after due court process, be recovered by the local authority in satisfaction of the debt. This could even occur where the resident has no income to contribute.

For example if at one time there was capital of say £100,000 of which £90,000 had been given away in the hope of avoiding care fees but the circumstances were such that the local authority could satisfy themselves of a significant avoidance intention, the £90,000 would be treated as notional capital, and the resident would be assessed accordingly as due to pay the whole weekly fee. In recovering what is due to them the local authority, having obtained a court order for payment of the debt, would be entitled first to claim **any** capital still in the hands of the resident regardless of how little it may be. Thereafter depending on the timing of the disposal they could use the **1983 Act** or insolvency law, as appropriate, to try to recover the capital which had been transferred to others.

Capital Disregards

1.19 Schedule 4 to the **1992 regulations** lists (mainly by reference to the Income Support (General) Regulations 1987 (S.I. No. 1967) as amended, many times) a number of capital assets which are not to be taken into account in the means assessment.

1.20 These **disregarded** items include:

(1) the **surrender value** of a life policy (i.e. what could be obtained if a current policy were cashed in) but do not include the **actual proceeds** of a policy which has matured or which has been surrendered; these like any other cash in hand or in the bank **are** taken into account **(paragraph 13 of Schedule 4)**;

(2) gifts **in kind** from a charity **(paragraph 17)**;

(3) **personal possessions** such as valuable paintings or antiques unless it can be proved they were purchased with the intention of reducing capital to avoid paying all or part of the local authority's claim for reimbursement of residential care fees **(paragraph 8)**;

(4) **certain rights which have not yet crystallised** as cash but which would have value to a third party, e.g. the right to receive outstanding payments due under a loan (but note that as the payments due under a loan are actually received, that money **is included in the assessment) (paragraph 12)**.

Know the Rules

1.21　Of greatest importance are the **exceptions** for **houses** or **land**. The value of the resident's dwelling is disregarded, sensibly, if his stay in residential care is only **temporary (paragraph 1)**. Its value is also ignored if it is occupied in whole or in part by:-

(1) the **resident's spouse** (provided they are not separated or divorced from each other) **(paragraph 2(1))**;

(2) a relative who is aged **60 or over**, or **under 16** and is a child whom the resident is liable to maintain, or who is incapacitated **(paragraph 2(2))**.

1.22　"**relative**" includes parents, parents in law, children or their spouses, step-parents, step-children, brothers, or sisters, and the spouses or partners of any of these, and grandparents, grandchildren, uncles, aunts, nephews, or nieces. It should be noted however that any of these relatives may themselves eventually have to go into residential care in which case the house will no longer be protected.

1.23　The local authority may also **at their discretion (paragraph 18 of Schedule 4)**, where it appears reasonable to do so, ignore the value of a house occupied by a relative (who does not fall into one of the above categories anyway, for example, the under 60-year-old spinster daughter looking after elderly ailing parents) who has given up a house to care for the person now in care or someone who played the part of "companion" to that person. Wherever there is a discretionary power there is always a corresponding requirement to exercise it in a rational manner after due consideration: a capricious or unjustifiable refusal by the local authority to exercise this discretion in favour of such a person could be challenged in the courts.

1.24　Judgement in the first case to challenge an alleged unreasonable exercise of this discretion was given in *R v Somerset County Council ex parte Harcombe* (1997) 37 B.M.L.R. 1. A son gave up his job in Australia to come home and remove his ailing mother from a residential care home. He resided with her and looked after her for two years until her condition deteriorated so much that she had to move back into residential care. Her income was insufficient to meet the care fees and the County Council decided that her house would have to be sold to meet the shortfall. In the meantime her son had briefly returned to Australia but finding no employment there came back to reside in the mother's house in the UK. He challenged the refusal of the County Council to exercise their discretion to allow him to continue to live in the house and not take it into account in the fees assessment (**paragraph 18 of Schedule 4**).

The County Council agreed to let him continue to occupy the house but refused to disregard its value in the fees assessment and took a charge over it so that the continually increasing fees deficit (with interest accruing from the date of the mother's death (section 24 of the **Health and Social Services and Social Security Adjudications Act 1983**)) eventually mounted up to over £25,000. The court decided that taking account of a particular circumstance of the case - that the son had gone back to Australia after caring for his mother, and that his eventual return to the UK was not in connection with caring for her - the Council had acted reasonably. The judge also emphasised that it was an important principle of legislation on residential care that those who could pay for it did so.

1.24.1 **Note:** if the mother had transferred the house to her son the Council could not have placed a charge on it as a charge is operative only against property owned by the person receiving care **(see 1.9(i))**; if the transfer had been more than six months prior to the second entry to care the Council could not have recovered its value from the son **(see 1.15)**; and if it could also have been demonstrated that in making the transfer she had no significant intention of avoiding payment of care fees the Council could not have regarded the transferred house as notional capital either **(see 1.14)**, in which case they could not have taken account of its value in the fees assessment, sued for any fees based on that value, or resorted to insolvency procedures to cut down the transaction.

1.25 The local authority have no power to force the sale of a house. Although they must (where no disregards apply) take the value of the house into account right from the day of entry to care and calculate the assessment accordingly, if the resident in care refuses to sell, the local authority have to wait until the resident changes his mind or dies. Then a legal charge, which they will have placed on the house either at the time of entry to care or when arrears mount up, can be operated to recoup out of the sale price what they are owed for unpaid care fees **(sections 22 and 23 of the Health and Social Services and Social Security Adjudications Act 1983)**.

Capital Jointly Held

1.26 Where a **house** is in co-ownership (but the **Schedule 4 disregard** does not apply, the co-owners not being married to each other, or married, but separated or for some other reason not in occupation) the question of the valuation of a share is a tricky one for which social security decisions provide some precedents. The **1992 Regulations** provide a valuation criterion for houses and other interests in land at **Regulation 27(2)** by introducing the concept of the willing buyer which differs from that which **Regulation 27(1)** applies to other capital assets such as savings. It should be possible to argue in **England and Wales** that the value of any share of a house is reduced (perhaps to nil) by the occupation of the other co-owner (if that is the case), the need for an application to court for an order to realise the share (which may be refused), and the unattractiveness to a purchaser of having to share ownership with another (but note that with regard to income support and other benefits the whole beneficial interest in capital jointly held is now treated as if it were held in equal shares of equal value (The Social Security Amendment (Capital)

Regulations 1998 (SI No 2250)). The co-owners would be the most likely purchasers but they would be well-advised not to demonstrate their interest, however keen, as that would enhance the valuation of the share being considered in the care fees assessment.

1.27 In **Scotland** the courts have no discretion to refuse an application by a co-owner to have the whole property sold and have the proceeds divided up in an action for sale and division. This is regarded as much more attractive to the notional willing purchaser of a share so that its value for assessment purposes will be put at much nearer its proportionate share of the normal market value of the house if sold as a whole (see *Upper Crathes Fishings Ltd v Baileys Executors* 1991 SC 30). Where Scottish co-owners are spouses and are subject to section 19 of the Matrimonial Homes (Family Protection) (Scotland) Act 1981 the court does have discretion to refuse an application for sale and division so that the value of a share in such a case could be reduced (perhaps to nil) as in England and Wales. However as the **Schedule 4 disregard** excludes the value of the house anyway where a spouse continues to reside in it, the matrimonial homes exception is likely to be of little relevance in the context of a local authority care fees assessment.

1.28 A half share of a savings account will be valued arithmetically by simple division as the question of disposal to a willing buyer does not arise (see **Regulation 27(1)** of the **1992 Regulations**). Where such capital is held jointly, one half of that capital will be assessed. It may therefore be advisable to split joint accounts into separate accounts as soon as possible as it is normally half the balance which is assessed **regardless of which joint holder has caused the increase or decrease in that balance.** An evidential problem regarding beneficial ownership may arise where a couple have a joint account but have acknowledged between themselves that one of them is entitled to more than a half share: this private acknowledgement may not be accepted in the local authority's assessment.

For example a couple may have £50,000 in a joint account but always have agreed privately that the wife's "share" is £40,000. If the husband goes into care he will be assessed as having £25,000 if the local authority insist on taking the joint account at its face value and refuse to recognise the unwritten private agreement with the wife. If on entry to care, or at some time prior to entry, they both, in acknowledgement of the private agreement, transfer £40,000 to an account in the wife's own name the husband could fall foul of the rules on deprivation of capital and still be assessed for the full £25,000 (of which £15,000 will be notional capital as it will have been transferred to the wife's name). Conversely if in the same circumstances the wife was the one to go into care it would be advantageous not to argue for recognition of the private agreement as she would be assessed as having only £25,000.

1.28.1 For an excellent discussion of this topic which is a model of clarity, commonsense, and sound law, and which suggests that a local authority cannot blindly apply the rule but must look at the evidence, see Social Security Commissioner's decision CIS/7097/95 (issued on **27th February 1997**). It is an income support case but the same principles can be applied to the interpretation of **regulation 27(1)** as although the income support legislation has been modified to nullify its effect in social security law there has been no comparable amendment to local authority law. The case concerned a joint current account the larger share of which consisted of the proceeds of a husband's National Savings Certificates. The daughter operated the account on behalf of her father to finance his nursing home fees and kept a careful note of all her transactions on his behalf. His wife who was the other joint account holder was held **not** to be entitled to any of the share which had come from her husband's savings certificates and which was now devoted to his care fees with the result that her capital became low enough for her to be entitled to income support.

The Commissioner said that where there is clear evidence of a contrary intention, such as that of using the joint account merely as a convenient way of handling money to be retained and used as the sole property of one of the parties, there is no reason in law or equity against giving effect to that intention. He added that between husband and wife such a contrary intention must be clearly and affirmatively proved if the presumption of joint beneficial ownership of the entirety is to be avoided, but that there was in the case under consideration the clearest possible evidence of a specific purpose that the father's savings should be used for his nursing home fees, and this evidence was supported by the careful accounting of the daughter and the fact that the direct debits were dealt with via the existing account.

Capital Held On Trust

1.29   A check should be made to determine if part of an elderly person's estate is held not by himself in his own legal right but in trust for another person. This will be obvious enough if there is a trust deed but not at all obvious if the trust is a **"secret"** or **"resulting"** trust not set out in writing. It commonly arises where late in life the elderly person has purchased a house with the assistance of children who have prospered better than the parents. The children may have contributed a major proportion of the purchase price and the question will be whether their contribution was a gift, a loan secured on the house, or a fund to be used by the parent as trustee for the children and to be invested in property, namely the house purchased for the parent's own use. Both for income support claims and for reduction of assets susceptible to the local authority means test it could be of great benefit to establish that the childrens' contribution was held by the parent as a trustee rather than donee because it will then be excluded from his estate for assessment purposes.

It may sometimes be possible to establish a trust arrangement even where the word "trust" never passed the lips of parties unsophisticated in the law (although

Know the Rules

in **Scotland** since 1st August 1995 a trust concerning any interest in land has had to be in writing).

1.30 All the facts and circumstances have to be taken into account. Regard should be had for example to leading cases such as *The Heritable Reversionery Company Ltd v Millar* (1892 18 R (HL) 43) a Scottish appeal which went to the House of Lords. Here a company had purchased property through its manager and instructed him to register it in his own name but privately to hold it in trust for the company. The manager subsequently went bankrupt and the question was whether his trustee in bankruptcy could claim the property for the benefit of his creditors in the face of a claim by the property company that despite the entry in the land register in the manager's name, they had privately agreed with him that he held it only in trust for the company. The court decided that although a purchase of the land by an innocent third party who relied on the entry in the land register could not have been cut down, the existence of the "secret" trust did prevent the trustee in bankruptcy from getting his hands on the property for the benefit of the manager's creditors.

1.31 There is a strong possibility that a similar ruling would be given where the DSS (for income support purposes) or a local authority (for assessment of means) tried to take into account property held under a similar secret or unstated trust arrangement but the variety of facts and circumstances which can emerge in these cases and the numerous technicalities of the law which can be summoned up for either side of the argument renders each case unique on its facts. To avoid that sort of dispute a properly advised son or daughter assisting elderly parents with house purchase will have such a trust arrangement not only in place but carefully set out in writing. It will however usually be simpler for the children to make their contribution by means of a loan secured on the property as the amount of such a loan will be deducted in the valuation for income support or local authority means assessment purposes.

1.32 In some cases it will be possible to show that the proportion not held in trust or not subject to a loan secured over the property is at the time of entry into care worth less than £10,000. Nevertheless in the commonest case where the house was formerly council owned and bought at a substantial discount under the right-to-buy schemes it is likely that the part "gifted" by the housing authority to the elderly person by way of discount will now be valued at far in excess of £10,000. Then it is essential to take the steps detailed in later chapters of this booklet to eliminate or minimise liability.

1.32.1 For further guidance on the question of **resulting trusts** (in **England and Wales**) reference should be made to Social Security Commissioner's decision CIS/030/93 (now *82/94). At paragraph 33 the Commissioner said that the direct contributions of the claimant's children to the purchase price of a house bought in 1958 would have created a resulting trust in their favour, which, in the absence of evidence to the contrary, would divide the beneficial interest in the house in proportion to their, and the claimant's, contributions to the purchase price. For example, if the claimant had, as a sitting tenant, received a discount on the market price of the house, that discount would have to be treated as a direct contribution to the purchase price. The claimant would then have held the house as legal owner on trust for the beneficiaries of the resulting trust in relation to the part of the beneficial interest not held by her. The creation of a resulting trust in that way, he added, does not rest on any **prior agreement or promise or assurance** as to what is to happen to the beneficial interest, but is created by the fact of the direct contributions to the purchase price. A resulting trust rests on a presumption, which is rebutted by proof of the **true intentions** of those who provided the purchase price.

The case of *Lawson v Coombes*, reported in the Times on 2nd December 1998, sheds a further socially interesting light on how a resultant trust may be created: there a married man who bought a house jointly with his mistress conveyed it into her sole name to prevent his wife from having any claim over it. The court held that when the relationship with the mistress ended the man was entitled not only to a declaration that she holds his half share in the property on a resulting trust for his benefit, but also to an order that it be sold and the proceeds divided between them.

Income Assessment

1.33   In assessing what the resident has to pay the local authority take **income** into account as well and the whole of the assessed income, apart from a few pounds allowed for personal expenses **(see 1.3)**, must be contributed to the cost of the residential care accommodation **(section 22** of the **National Assistance Act 1948,** and **section 87** of the **Social Work (Scotland) Act 1968)**. Income includes occupational pensions, most state benefits, and income from annuities and trusts (but not income generated by a discretionary trust if dispensed by the trustees in exercise of their discretion).

Disregarded Income

1.34   Income from capital of between £10,000 and £16,000 is treated in a special way: the actual interest or dividend is not taken into account but is treated as capital **(regulation 22(4))** and the **tariff income** calculation referred to above in **1.16** is applied to the whole capital, usually much to the resident's detriment as he will have to reduce it to provide sums equal to that imaginary income. However where capital (which itself may be wholly or partly notional) is treated as **"disregarded"** the **actual** income it produces is taken into account. For example the capital value of the right to have a loan repaid is disregarded but the interest payments received from that disregarded asset will count.

Know the Rules

Some minor income is disregarded e.g. a Christmas bonus paid with state benefits. Further examples of disregarded income are to be found in **Schedules 2** and **3** to the **National Assistance (Assessment of Resources) Regulations 1992 (S.I. No 2977)**. Other income which is disregarded are payments made by **third parties** (e.g. by a discretionary trust) to make good **arrears** of fees for residential accommodation if paid directly to the local authority **(see regulations 16(4)** and **17(4)** and **(5)** of the **1992 Regulations**).

Deprivation of Income

1.35 It is not possible to evade the assessment by covenanting to pay income to someone else unless it can be shown that there was **no significant intention of depriving oneself** of the income simply to qualify for a reduced assessment. Therefore if someone now resident in residential care has covenanted some or all of his income to a relative ostensibly to pay for, say, the relative's education the local authority will want to be satisfied that the purpose was genuine.

1.36 A resident can be treated as having income of which he has deprived himself for the purpose of reducing the local authority assessment of what he has to pay if it can be shown that an intention to reduce or avoid liability played a significant part in the decision to make the transfer. The concept of **notional income** is provided for in **regulation 17(1)** of the **1992 Regulations**. As with deprivation of capital **these regulations themselves** provide no power to claw back such transferred income from third parties.

Income Recovery

1.37 Where there has been such a transfer of cash the local authority may use **section 21** of the **Health and Social Services and Social Security Adjudications Act 1983** to transfer liability to the person to whom the cash is being passed because it then becomes an asset in that person's hands (but the six month time limit on the date of transfer, or on successive dates of transfers, still applies). That person will then have to pay the local authority for that part of the residential care fees assessed as being covered by the income of which the resident has deprived himself.

Spousal Liability

1.38 There is one other source of income to part of which the local authority will lay claim. That is a **spouse's income** because under **section 42** of the **National Assistance Act 1948** spouses are liable to maintain each other. However the principal of mutual support has now been more fairly applied so that where one spouse with an occupational pension (as from **8th April 1996**) or personal pension scheme pension, or retirement annuity (as from **7th April 1997**) is in care, and the other is not, only **one half** of the occupational pension etc can be taken into account in the assessment of means by the local authority **(Paragraph 10A** of **Schedule 3** to the **1992 Regulations)**. This concession however does not apply to parties who are not married (although in **Scotland** where there has been no formal ceremony it may be possible to claim eligibility by proving the existence of an irregular marriage based on habit and repute - marriages constituted on that basis are accepted by DSS as establishing entitlement to widow's benefit for example).

1.39 It is useful to remember too that the amount a spouse has to contribute can, in the absence of agreement, be determined only by a court (**section 43(2)** of the **1948 Act**). The local authority have no powers either to ascertain the **spouse's** capital or income, or to decide how much should be paid (this being another example of how the local authority's **means** assessment powers can differ from those of the DSS assessing **eligibility** for income support where the capital and income of both spouses or partners are taken into account directly by DSS and the benefit computed accordingly).

2

Dispose of the Assets

Where there is insufficient income to meet the whole care costs, but there are capital assets in the background, the local authority will claim them or their value in reimbursement of the balance of the care fees for the accommodation which the local authority provide or arrange. If such a situation is identified as likely to arise immediate consideration should be given to finding a safe destination to which the assets can be transferred. However before any action is taken the elderly person and his family should consider whether or not he will be able to pay for residential care wholly out of his own income. If there is likely to be sufficient income there will be no need to protect the assets by disposal as the income will pay the care fees and thereby exclude local authority involvement.

Self Financing

2.2   In some cases the net income after tax from the state pension, occupational pension, and interest on savings and investment, together with the income which can be generated from the house which the person will no longer occupy will be sufficient to pay for the desired standard of care if he has to go into a residential home. If it is reasonably certain that enough income will be available for a sufficient length of time the expense of taking avoiding action by setting up a trust can be saved if the only consideration is the possibility of loss of assets to the local authority.   There are however other good reasons for putting the family assets into trust, such as to prevent their subsequent dissipation by dissolute members of the family on succession, or their inadvertent loss by an elderly person persuaded into unwise remarriage, or contracts offered by unscrupulous salesmen.

Attendance Allowance

2.3   One potential source of additional income is **attendance allowance**. Many elderly people fail to claim this as they think that it is available only to those who actually engage someone to look after them. In fact the allowance is available regardless of how it is spent or saved. Eligibility simply depends on an assessment of physical condition such as ability to get in or out of bed or go to the toilet unaided. Anyone who requires nursing care (as opposed to simple residential care) should qualify.

Dispose of the Assets

2.4 The allowance is **non-means tested, non contributory,** and **tax free.** The important thing to remember is that it can remain payable even after entry to the residential home if the person in receipt of the allowance is not entitled to income support or housing benefit, **and** the whole of the cost of the accommodation is met out of his own resources, or by relatives or by a charity. This applies regardless of whether the accommodation is wholly privately provided or its provision is secured by a local authority under **Part III (section 26** of the **National Assistance Act 1948 (in England and Wales)** or **Part IV (section 59(2)(c))** of the **Social Work (Scotland) Act 1968 (in Scotland)**. The other requirement is that the residential home is not owned or managed by a local authority, an increasingly likely situation nowadays. These requirements are set out in **regulations 7** and **8** of the **Social Security (Attendance Allowance) Regulations 1991 (S.I. No. 2740)** as amended.

2.5 However where the cost of care is met by the local authority and is then recouped out of the resident's assets when he dies (e.g. by a charge on his house under **sections 22** or **23** of the **Health and Social Services and Social Security Adjudications Act 1983** - see **1.9 (i)**) so that although at the end of the day the cost of care is **effectively** met not by the local authority but by the resident's estate, attendance allowance is **not** payable. For the allowance to be payable the care costs have to be met directly **as they arise** by the resident, relatives, etc (Social Security Commissioners Decision CA/11185/95).

2.6 A judgement issued by the House of Lords in *Steane v Chief Adjudication Officer and Another* [1996] 1WLR1195(HL) is of particular importance (in **England and Wales** at any rate as it interprets section **21(1)(a)** of the **1948 Act**, whereas the comparable provision in **Scotland** is the very differently worded **section 12** of the **1968 Act**). That case confirmed that even where the local authority have **power** (the "may be borne" provision in **Regulation 7(1)(c)** of the **1991 Regulations)** to subsidise accommodation, but do not **in fact** do so, because other arrangements are in place, attendance allowance is still payable; and that a person pays the "whole cost" (as required by **Regulation 8(6)(b)**) of his accommodation if he pays the charge fixed for residents in respect of his individual accommodation. Residents are still to be treated as paying the whole cost even where from time to time the residential home has received grants out of public (national or local) funds.

This judgement also confirms a loophole (known as the "Boyd loophole" having been named after the gentleman who discovered it) which enables **both** attendance allowance **and** income support (by those who qualify for the latter) to be claimed: the "may be borne" provision in **Regulation 7(1)(c)** cannot operate where relatives or a charity top up the difference between the care fee and what is received by way of attendance allowance and income support as the accommodation is then "otherwise available" (i.e. privately arranged).

Dispose of the Assets

2.7 One unfortunate side effect of Steane was that the "otherwise available" argument could be used by local authorities to justify nonintervention on their part until the person's resources had been all but totally exhausted where care had initially been privately secured: *R v Sefton Metropolitan Borough Council* (Times Law Report, March 27 1997). In that case a lady had used her own assets to fund private care until they fell below £16,000 and the local authority's refusal to carry out an assessment at that stage was upheld by the lower court on the grounds that there was no care need for them to meet so long as the private care continued to be provided, and that their own resources were strained. That decision was overturned in the Court of Appeal so that the original intention of the legislation was reinstated: the local authority must first carry out an assessment of need and then have regard to the statutory figure of £16,000 in assessing means.

To make doubly sure **section 21** of the **National Assistance Act 1948 (for England and Wales)** and **section 12** of the **Social Work (Scotland) Act 1968** were amended by the Community Care (Residential Accommodation) Act 1998 which came into force on **11th August 1998**. Its provisions prevent local authorities from wrongly taking into account any part of the resident's capital below the £16,000 and £10,000 limits set in subordinate legislation.

Dangerous Disposals

2.8 Not surprisingly many elderly persons and their relatives have sought, and are still seeking, professional advice on ways of putting their assets **beyond the reach of the local authority.** Some think the solution lies in gifting assets to relatives or friends just before entry to care. Nothing could be further from the truth. Even where property or income has been transferred to third parties the local authority can claw their value back **if they were transferred with an avoidance intention** at less than their market value within a certain period **(see 1.15)**, or treat them as notional capital on which to base an enhanced assessment regardless of when they were transferred **(see 1.14)**.

2.9 In any case there are other dangers in making a simple **transfer of property to relatives** no matter how close-knit a family may be. Even if the recipient of the gift can be trusted absolutely he or she may be vulnerable: for example, on divorce a spouse may claim a substantial share of the other spouse's assets. These would include the gift or a share of it. Thus the resident could see assets he saved for the benefit of his successors disappearing with the departing spouse to the benefit of some new family. Many would prefer to see the assets taken by the local authority than have them dissipated in this way.

2.10 Gifted assets can be lost in other ways. The son or daughter may become a compulsive gambler or alcoholic. He or she may be in debt. The transferred assets could quickly disappear into the hands of bookmakers, publicans, or creditors. And if the assets were given away on the informal understanding that they would still be used for the donor's needs and accommodation prior to going into care there is a risk that the donee will not keep to his word. Parents and children may be on good terms when the house and other assets are transferred, but circumstances and attitudes often change.

One lady gave her house to her daughter on condition that she would look after her there for the rest of her days. Instead, the daughter evicted her. The Court of Appeal upheld a Social Security Commissioner's decision that the daughter, having breached one of the conditions attached to the gift, did not own it at all but held it on trust for her mother. The consequence of that finding was that the mother, not having effectively rid herself of the property, breached the capital limits for eligibility for income support, although having been evicted by the daughter, she had lost her home in fact, if not in law, and had only a remote chance of ever having it restored to her *(Ellis v Chief Adjudication Officer*, Times Law Report, 14th May 1997). It should also be remembered that the assets transferred could increase the **recipient's** income or capital tax liabilities, or decrease or eliminate his eligibility for state benefits.

2.11 Another consideration is that the person who gives away assets may never actually go into residential care. The frustration of the local authority's potential claim will have proved unnecessary, and the risk will have been borne for nothing, not to mention the loss of independence.

Discretionary Trusts

2.12 The solution therefore for many people is to set up a trust in which they will be both a trustee and a beneficiary, and transfer the assets to it, rather than to their fickle kin, but it has to be a special kind of trust, namely a **discretionary trust.** An ordinary trust will not do as a beneficiary under such a trust has a right to the proceeds and even if he elects not to claim them the local authority will still take them into account and treat them as **notional capital (see 1.14)**. The assets of a discretionary trust and the income they produce however cannot be taken into account by the local authority in assessing what the truster as a resident in residential care can pay. Furthermore as ownership of the assets has passed from the resident as an individual to himself and others **as trustees** they cannot be claimed or taken into account by the local authority if he has acted with demonstrably "innocent" intention.

2.13 A trust is set up when one party, the "truster" or "settlor", transfers all or part of his assets to one or more other persons as "trustees", with instructions on how they are to look after these assets, what to do with any income they produce, and how to distribute them when a certain event, such as the truster's death, occurs.

2.14 The important difference between an ordinary trust and a discretionary one is that although all of these instructions may be given to the trustees they will also be given **absolute discretion**, set out on the face of the trust deed, as to

Dispose of the Assets

when or whether they should ever pay anything out to the truster as beneficiary or any of the other beneficiaries. The essential feature of such a trust is that no single beneficiary has any enforceable entitlement and the trustees decide from time to time which of the beneficiaries is to receive a share of the income or capital. The choice of such a trust as the destination for the assets provides protection against the irrationalities and foibles of old age and the mistakes and misfortunes which may assail the coming generation but it does not by itself provide any protection from the local authority's powers. **Timing, evidence of intention, and the trust purposes (as these last may form part of the evidence about intention)** have always to be carefully considered. In a dispute with the local authority over the intention behind a transfer, it may be easier to demonstrate an "innocent" intention where the transferee is a trust rather than an individual **(see Ch 4)**.

2.15 The **professional fees** and outlays incurred in transferring an estate worth £100,000 (say £75,000 for a modest house and £25,000 in savings) will amount to about 1% of the whole. They will be proportionally more for a small estate and less for a larger one. Most people will consider it well worthwhile spending £1,000 to help the family retain £100,000 in their own hands rather than let it pass to a local authority. It is also worth noting that the more that passes to a trust during one's lifetime the less expensive legal work that will be required in connection with one's executry at the end of the day.

2.16 Although it is possible for the layman to draft the trust deed himself, the advantage of engaging a professional is that he not only has specialist knowledge, but also is covered by professional indemnity insurance to compensate any client who suffers because of a gap in that knowledge. The draft deed at **page 71** should be helpful but should not be relied on as covering all the eventualities which may have to be considered in any particular case. No-one can be absolutely sure of the effect of any deed until a court has pronounced on it if any of the parties to it, or affected by it, disagree about its interpretation. Fortunately the majority of trust deeds quietly serve their purpose, sometimes through many generations, and are never in contention.

2.17 A trust, like most man-made creations, has to be looked after. Where the estate is a simple one consisting of a house (which may be turned into cash on the entry to care) and savings accounts, the reasonably literate and numerate layman may have no difficulty in recording the trustees' decisions (regarding investments and disbursements), producing a simple set of accounts, and making an annual tax return. However where investments are more complicated and none of the trustees is willing or able to undertake the administration of the trust a professional adviser has to be engaged. An estimate of the annual fee should be made before the trust solution is adopted, and a decision taken whether the value of the estate being protected is worth the expense. There is no legal reason why a man and wife should not set up one trust for their property jointly. This would be particularly apt where some or all of their matrimonial property is held in joint names. They can both together entrust all their property to trustees and could both, with others such as their children, be trustees and potential beneficiaries. With only one, rather than two, trusts to set up and administer there should then be a saving in charges.

Irrevocability

2.18 Ensuring that the trust cannot be revoked is very important. It is essential to state explicitly that the truster regards his act in setting up the trust as **irrevocable**. That in itself however may not be enough if the only beneficiary of the trust is the truster himself. It is essential therefore to name other beneficiaries on whom the act of setting up the trust confers rights. These beneficiaries can insist in the face of any demands by the local authority for revocation that the truster conferred irrevocable rights on them on which they now rely - they can say this even if they are not currently receiving any payments from the trust. The existence of a trust fund for their benefit if the trustees choose so to exercise their discretionary powers is sufficient. Furthermore as no identifiable part of the trust fund will have been allocated specifically for the benefit of the truster the local authority cannot insist that part of the trust be revoked or that some of its funds be handed back when he goes into residential care.

Timing

2.19 It is the **date of actual transfer** of the assets to the trust which counts for assessment purposes, not the date the trust is set up. The **six month time limit** imposed by section **21(1)(b)(i)** of the **1983 Act** still applies even where the transfer of assets has been to a trust rather than to a natural person. If the transfer of the assets to the trust takes place **within the six month period, or after the entry to care,** and with the intention of avoiding care fees, the local authority can claim them or their value back from the trust just as they could from any other party who receives them from the resident at less than their market value. The local authority could also treat the transferred assets as notional capital if there was no fees debt (thanks to relatives making good the shortfall), but a reason was required to refuse an abatement of, or contribution to, the fees. If the transfer takes place **more than six months** prior to the entry to care and there is evidence of an avoidance intention the value of the transferred assets cannot be reclaimed by the local authority (except possibly following insolvency proceedings) but they will be treated as notional capital.

It should be remembered however that, contrary to popular belief, **there is no fixed period within which transfers cannot be defended, or beyond which transfers are immune from challenge**. What counts is evidence of intention.

Dispose of the Assets

If an innocent intention can be demonstrated a transfer which takes places even within weeks of entry to care may be successfully defended. On the other hand assets which were the subject of a transfer which took place years ago cannot escape being treated as notional capital by the local authority if there is clear evidence still extant of an avoidance intention at that time. It will usually be advantageous nevertheless to transfer assets as long as possible before the entry to care, if only because the evidence of intention will become tarnished by age.

Intention

2.20 Care should be taken not to say anything about avoiding residential care costs either in the trust deed or in ancillary correspondence, such as correspondence between a professional adviser and the client. Indeed it may be imprudent to use the services of firms whose **sole** services appear to consist of assisting in the disposal of assets so as to avoid liability as the use of such a firm could by itself be evidence of intention. And the fact that this book has ever been seen or read should never be mentioned. (It is worth noting that where a claimant who is accused of deprivation of assets in order to found a claim for income support can convincingly deny all knowledge of the income support deprivation rules it will be accepted that the deprivation took place for some other reason (Social Security Commissioners Decision, CIS/24/1990). It is possible that the courts would take the same attitude in dealing with allegations of deliberate deprivation in a case concerning a residential care fees assessment, but see *Yule v South Lanarkshire Council (No 2)* at **page 92 infra**).

2.21 In the context of avoiding loss of assets to local authorities an exhibition of apparent ignorance of the deprivation rules could be helpful even if the entry to care takes place **within** six months of the transfer of assets as a claim might still be denied if there is convincing evidence that there was nothing further from the truster's mind at the time and he had other good reason for setting up the trust and transferring his assets (section **21(1)(b)** of the **Health and Social Services and Social Security Adjudications Act 1983**). The "knowingly" requirement in this provision could be a rather difficult one for the local authority to prove in the face of stout denials of knowledge. (**In Scotland** however in some cases getting round the requirements of **section 21** may be of no avail if the circumstances are such that the unfair preference provisions of the **insolvency** legislation can be invoked by the local authority because intention is not taken into account in a **statutory** challenge to a transaction within the six month period - **see Ch 5).**

2.22 In the calculation of notional income and capital under **regulations 17** and **25** of the **National Assistance (Assessment of Resources) Regulations 1992** evidence of any significant intention to avoid liability for fees will be taken into account by the local authority in considering any transaction which took place at any time.

Dispose of the Assets

2.23 Obviously the client who has had competent professional advice will not be able to plead ignorance of the rules. A properly advised client would have to be told about the deprivation rules and significant intention precedents and thereafter could not plead ignorance, but this would be done as part of comprehensive advice which would cover **both** the possible destinations for the assets (whether children, a trust, etc) **and** a range of reasons ("innocent" as well as "incriminating") for their transfer (for example for better management of the property, **or** to protect it from the depredation of possibly dissolute successors, or their creditors, **or** the protection of assets from claims by a local authority providing residential care). It would then be up to the client to say which purpose should be stated in his trust deed, and it would **not** be unethical for his agent **not** to cross examine him on the genuineness of his stated intentions.

An ethically difficult situation does arise when a client boldly announces that he wants to dispose of his assets for the specific reason of denying them to the local authority. That would be akin to the client on a criminal charge admitting his guilt to his agent but instructing him to put forward a substantive defence in court. The other thing to bear in mind is that all communications between a solicitor and client are confidential: a local authority trying to establish significant intention would have to rely on correspondence with others - if they could get at it - and remarks made, for example to social workers, etc (but see *Barclays Bank v Eustice* [1995] 4 AER 511 if fraud is alleged).

Purposes

2.24 The **preamble** to the trust deed sets out who is the granter of the deed, i.e., the truster, and who are the persons to whom the truster's assets are being entrusted, i.e. the trustees. It will also state briefly the reason why the truster is setting up the trust, e.g. "wishing to make proper provision for myself and my children" (and will definitely not make any reference to the avoidance of liability for care fees!)

2.25 The preamble will give the full names and addresses of the truster, trustees, and beneficiaries and it may contain some formal provisions about **acceptance of office** by the trustees, their **declinature** or **death,** and what is to constitute a **quorum.** It will also include the **transfer** by the truster to the trustees of a nominal sum of say £5 and state that it and any other assets transferred by the truster or anyone else at any time are to be held by the trustees for the "following purposes". These purposes are then set out in numbered clauses and should include the following:

2.26 **First:** for payment of any expenses connected with the **administration** of the trust and the carrying out of its purposes;

2.27 **Second:** directions to the trustees including the all important **discretionary**

Dispose of the Assets

element. The trustees will be told for example that they may at any time, and from time to time pay, apply, allocate, or appoint all or any part of the free income or capital of the trust and any income for the benefit of all or one or more of the beneficiaries.

2.28 How or what or when is explicitly stated to be a matter for their own discretion. And in doing so they will also be empowered to attach such conditions, limitations and qualifications as they think fit. A time limit during which they may do all of this may be imposed: for example their powers, and the trust, may be brought to an end by the truster's death. A time limit of that kind would be appropriate in the context of the truster's estate being put in trust to avoid the assets being seized for payment of residential care fees as the funds are protected during the truster's life by the trust and no longer require that protection after he is dead (as the trust will contain a destination - other than the local authority - for the funds remaining on the truster's death). The trust deed should, as far as possible, follow a standard style and contain certain essential provisions and directions if it is to succeed in its purpose of protecting the truster's assets.

2.29 It must (in the context of putting the truster's assets beyond the reach of a claim for reimbursement of residential care fees) state explicitly that (1) the trustees have **absolute discretion** as to what they do with the trust funds and the income these funds produce and (2) the setting up of the trust and the transfer of assets to it is **irrevocable.** The truster can be reassured that this does not mean a complete and utter surrender of his property to the whims of his trustees as the inclusion of clauses of this nature does not entitle the trustees to engage in a free-for-all with the assets **(see 2.31 - 2.33).**

Choosing The Trustees

2.30 The **choice of trustees** is a very personal one to which much thought should be given. The simplest and safest choice may be the truster himself, one or more of his own adult children, and a professional adviser of his own choosing. Being a trustee in one's own trust provides the reassurance of having some say in decisions about how the trust funds should be invested or disbursed - at least until one becomes mentally incapable of doing so which event may or may not coincide with the date of entry into care. A professional adviser provides an independent element, although of course the trust funds will have to bear his annual fee, but sound financial advice could ensure that the trust funds grow in value each year. An adult child who is appointed as trustee can also be a beneficiary under the trust. There is no legal objection too in the present context to the truster himself being both his own trustee and one of the beneficiaries who may, at the trustees' discretion, benefit under the trust deed. One benefit the truster will seek is the right to remain in occupation of the house donated to the discretionary trust but it is essential that this is left, on the face of it, at least, to the discretion of the trustees.

Dispose of the Assets

Controlling The Trustees

2.31 The disposal of assets to a discretionary trust, thereby putting them beyond personal control, may give some cause for concern regarding the safety of the arrangement. Some comfort can be gained from the fact that the use of trusts to protect property is a time-honoured one. In addition although the trustees may have absolute discretion trust law and the provisions of the trust deed do apply certain stringent controls to them.

2.32 **First**, the scope of their discretion is **limited by the naming of beneficiaries.** These will normally include the truster, and selected members of his family, for whose benefit the trustees will be entrusted to hold the assets. The discretionary qualification allows them to decide whether to pay out, or not pay out, any or all of the capital or income to any or all of these beneficiaries but they cannot squander it in other directions.

2.33 **Second**, in all they do trustees are **bound by law to act in good faith** so that assets held in trust by discretionary trustees for named beneficiaries are better protected from fraud or loss than assets transferred to children or other relatives: none of the restrictions which apply to the conduct of trustees apply to the conduct of children or relatives.

Declarations

2.34 A trust need not contain any further provisions or directions to the trustees unless the truster's circumstances are very unusual. It is normal however to add certain "declarations" which will make life easier for the trustees and which could save them the trouble, and the trust the expense, of having to go to court to have the trust conditions or purposes modified to meet changes in circumstances which were not envisaged by the truster when he set up the trust. The draft at **page 72** gives examples of some common declarations.

Power of Attorney

2.35 It is a good idea (subject at present to careful consideration of *Yule v South Lanarkshire Council (No. 2)* - see **page 93** *infra)* for the truster also to execute a **Power of Attorney** at the same time as he executes the trust deed as, although most of his assets will then be looked after by his trustees he may personally retain up to £10,000 under the current rules which the local authority are not allowed to take into account in their assessment. If the truster eventually becomes mentally incapable of managing his own affairs the person appointed to act under the power of attorney will be able to transfer any residual assets to the trust, so that the trustees can augment the trust funds and the income they produce. **Section 71** of the **Law Reform (Miscellaneous Provisions) (Scotland) Act 1990** and **section 1** of the **Enduring Powers of Attorney Act 1985 (for England and Wales)** provide for powers of attorney to survive the mental incapacity of the granter or donor.

3

Postpone the Day

If entry to care is imminent or takes place earlier than expected, consideration should be given to using the strategies outlined below. These could avoid, or at least postpone, a challenge by the local authority.

Postponing Entry To Part III Accommodation

3.1 The six month time limit in the **1983 Act** runs back from the date of entry into, not simply, "residential care" in the popular sense of the words, but **Part III accommodation (see section 21(1)(a) and (8))**. If the setting up of the trust and transfer of funds to it has been left too late, or is otherwise overtaken by events, so that the entry to care takes place before the six months is up, and there is a risk that the local authority will be able to prove an avoidance intention behind the disposal, if funds are available consideration should be given to arranging residential care for the requisite period (the balance of the time limit still to run) on a completely **private basis** with no local authority involvement. All or part of the cost could be met out of pensions, interest on capital, the assets and income of the trust, and possibly attendance allowance.

3.2 Once a clear six months have run from the date the assets were transferred, the local authority can be asked to do their need and means assessments, which will then have to be based on whatever assets the resident has retained out of the trust diminished by whatever he has expended on private care. (Eligibility for income support during the temporary period in totally private care should also be explored as DSS will not take the value of the house into account for at least six months if steps are being taken to sell it.) The same procedure could perhaps be used to thwart a possible challenge under the insolvency laws (particularly where **section 341(2)** of the **Insolvency Act 1986** could apply in **England and Wales**) but then the burden of privately financing non-Part III accommodation would be rather heavy as a two year period could be involved. The other drawback is that the resident would possibly have to change to another home after the local authority intervention.

It should not be forgotten of course that if the main reason for adopting the strategy outlined above at **3.1** was a fear that the local authority could prove an avoidance intention, they could still use the same evidence to treat the disposed of assets as notional capital. Their right to reclaim the value of the transferred assets from transferees under **section 21** of the **1983 Act** will however have been thwarted.

"Pseudo Part III" Accommodation

3.3 An assertion by a local authority that accommodation is, or was, provided under **Part III** should be closely scrutinised following the House of Lords judgment in *Quinn (for Harris deceased) and Others v Chief Adjudication Officer and Another* [1996] 1 WLR 1184 (HL). In that case the Lords decided that where a local authority do not provide the accommodation themselves but secure its provision by a voluntary body under **section 26** of the **1948 Ac**t there is **no Part III arrangement** if the financial arrangements between the local authority and the care provider, provided for in **section 26(2)** of the **1948 Act,** have not been made. Strange as it may seem such a situation did arise in a number of cases, especially where a local authority-owned home passed with its residents to a private provider.

3.4 Following *Quinn* there is an advantage for the local authority in that a higher proportion of an eligible resident's fees will be met by central government through income support where a Part III arrangement cannot be proved. The disadvantage for the local authority in such a situation is that if there is no Part III arrangement all the statutory rights and obligations in **sections 21 to 23** of the **1983 Act** become unenforceable against a resident who has assets as they all depend on the existence of a Part III arrangement.

3.5 Where a resident has left the disposal of his assets too late and he finds himself in accommodation to which Part III cannot at present apply due to the absence of a **section 26(2)** financial arrangement between the local authority and the independent body which provides it, there is an opportunity for him to protect his assets by transferring them immediately and letting the six month time limit run. As the local authority may move to put things right as soon as they become aware of the defects in the arrangements a resident in such a situation may be well advised to delay stating explicitly why he is refusing to pay until as much as possible of the six months has run, but a refusal to pay, combined with inquiries about the nature of the arrangements, will put the local authority on the alert.

3.6 This escape route should be available in **Scotland too** as section **87(4)** of the **Social Work (Scotland) Act 1968** imports "arrangements" from **section 26** of the **1948 Act without qualification.**

3.7 For accommodation to qualify as Part III/IV it has to be "arranged" in Scotland as elsewhere (**section 59** of the **1968 Act**). In one case, (Social Security Commissioners Decision CSIS/453/95), where the DSS were in dispute with the

Postpone the Day

local authority over which should contribute most, financially, to the care of some long term residents who had transferred from a local authority residence to a private one, the DSS were unable to prove the existence of a contract between the local authority and the new independent care provider (i.e. no Part IV arrangement), with the result that DSS had to bear a greater, and the local authority a lesser, share of the fees burden. Therefore where a local authority claim that accommodation is Part III or Part IV accommodation it is always worth checking that all the statutory and contractual elements for arranging such accommodation have been complied with. Lacking these, Part III or Part IV accommodation arrangements may only be masquerading as such so that those availing themselves of such defective arrangements are not caught by the enforcement provisions in **section 21** etc of the **1983 Act.**

Domiciliary Care

3.8   A knowledge of the rules governing provision of, and payment for, local authority **home help services** provided in the home can be useful as such care usually precedes the entry to residential care and is means tested. Obviously one of the best strategies for avoiding, or postponing, a residential care fees debt, is to stay at home and be cared for there as long as possible.

3.9   In **England** and **Wales** local authorities are empowered to assess a person's need for domiciliary services under **section 47** of the **National Health Service and Community Care Act 1990** which is the same provision as empowers them to assess needs for residential care services. Their powers to charge for domiciliary services however are different from, and less intimidating than, those which can be applied for the recovery of residential care fees. Section 17 of the **Health and Social Services and Social Security Adjudications Act 1983** empowers a local authority which provides a domiciliary care service (under any of various enactments) to recover such charge as they consider "reasonable". In **Scotland** the comparable powers of assessment, provision, and charging are found in **sections 12, 12A, 14,** and **87** of the **Social Work (Scotland) Act 1968.**

3.10   The interpretation of "reasonable" varies from one authority to another and apparently can be applied to the reasonableness of the charge both in relation to what is provided **and** the means of the person who receives the provision (compare for example **subsections (1)** and **(3)(b)** of **section 17** of the **1983 Act).** However if the service is provided and not paid for the only method of recovery available to the local authority is a debt recovery action in the courts. In contrast to the position with recovery of residential care fees they have no statutory powers to place a charge on property or to recover assets which have been donated to others. Nevertheless some authorities adopt in their means test for domiciliary care the same rules as to **assessment** of capital and income as are applied in a means test for payment of residential care fees.

3.11   Such authorities may attempt to take the value of the house in which the recipient of the service lives into account and collect **"tariff income"** related to its value but this should be strenuously resisted as unreasonable and contested through the complaints procedure **(see 4.10)** In making an assessment for **residential** care fees it may be reasonable to take the value of the house into account not only because the rules permit it but because on the departure to care of a sole owner the house can be sold and the proceeds devoted to the fees. Where however services are by their very nature to be provided in that house the value of the house can make no contribution to the charges which are made for the services. The same argument however could not be deployed with regard to other property owned by the recipient of the services unless there were some other strong reasons preventing its sale.

3.12 It should be remembered that if a local authority do attempt to use the capital part of the residential care fees assessment regime to assess means for domiciliary care services a prior disposal of assets will be as effective here as it will be against a means assessment for residential care, and will not be subject to any rule which enables a local authority to reclaim transferred assets or to treat them as notional capital, as these rules do not apply to the provision of domiciliary services.

3.13 Although policy demands that people in need of care should be cared for in the community for as long as possible most local authorities being short of funds will eventually weigh the cost of providing services to a person in his own home against that of having him in a residential care home. The latter choice will not necessarily cost them more. Suppose the "reasonable" charging regime imposed by the authority for domiciliary care produces a maximum contribution of £35 per week but the needs of the elderly person eventually increase so that meeting them costs the local authority £100 per week. A place in a residential care home might cost £350 per week but the charging regime which the local authority have to impose in the means assessment for such care takes almost all, rather than only part, of the resident's income **and** the value of his house and other assets into account. Together, they could result in a contribution equal to the whole cost. In such a case therefore a move to residential care could save the local authority £65 per week. Beware of pressure at this stage from the local authority for a move to residential care. If the move is not welcomed by the person receiving the domiciliary care this is certainly the time to reveal that the person's assessable assets have already been disposed of in a manner which puts them safely beyond the reach of the local authority's powers so that the authority will in fact have to bear the major part of the residential care fee (i.e. the whole care fee less any contribution from the resident's income such as a pension).

3.14 Until recently it would also have been useful to quote *R. v Islington London Borough Council ex parte Rixon* (Times, April 17 1996): that case established, for the space of a year, that an assessment should be based on the person's **need**, not the local authority's availability of **resources**, and that looking backwards over the shoulder at these resources should play no part in an honest assessment of whether or not the person can continue to live at home. This perfectly reasonable approach was overturned by a majority of only 3 to 2 judges in the House of Lords in *Regina v Gloucestershire County Council and Another, ex parte Barry* [1997] 2 AER 1. That case was about the proper interpretation of section 2(1) of the Chronically Sick and Disabled Persons Act 1970 but the same principal is likely to be applied to the interpretation of the domiciliary care provisions in the **1990 Act (England and Wales)** and the **1968 Act (Scotland)**.

4

Defend a Deprivation

When the relevant provisions of the National Health Service and Community Care Act 1990 were brought into force on 1st April 1993, and for some years thereafter, the main consideration for elderly people with assets but modest incomes was to find some way of disposing of the assets so as to put them beyond the reach of a local authority care fees assessment. That will remain an important concern for many people for some years yet, but others who did dispose of assets and who are now in care are being faced with a new problem. Local authorities are increasingly inclined to challenge these disposals with a view to either retrieving the value of the assets to pay the care fees, or treating them as notional capital on which an enhanced assessment, or a refusal by the local authority to contribute, can be based.

Arguing the Case

4.2 Where a local authority have clear evidence of an avoidance purpose or intention associated with a disposal (such as may be found in correspondence or, less persuasive, have been mentioned to social workers or home helps) they will refer to it in the means assessment or subsequent correspondence. In such cases a straightforward assessment of the available evidence will show whether the local authority's claim can be successfully defended or not. However if they use any of the following arguments it can be assumed that they have no such conclusive evidence and the weakness of their case will be easier to demonstrate.

Local authority argument (1)

- when the elderly person gave away his assets he was already in poor health and must (by that very fact alone) have been contemplating entry to residential care sometime in the near future: the donation must therefore have been for the purpose of decreasing a possible liability to pay for care fees.

(i) This is a weak argument based on a *non sequitur*, or two, but it was used by the local authority in *Yule (No.2)*- **see 4.4** and **page 93 *infra*,** and accepted by the court, although poor health at the date of transfer of assets by itself provides no evidence of purpose or intention or knowledge. The explanation for a transfer could be that the elderly person had become

Defend a Deprivation

too frail to be troubled with the maintenance and administration of his property while stoutly resisting any suggestion that he is in need of residential care. (A statement to this effect in a trust deed setting up a trust to which property has been transferred will support this argument, whereas a transfer to a relative who is not renowned for his administrative skills e.g. a teenager, would tend to negate it).

(ii) In addition there may be evidence that the elderly person had made arrangements for a friend or relative to look after him, or even had no more than a reasonable expectation of such assistance, so that there would be no question of incurring, far less avoiding, liability for care fees **(see also (3)(ii) below).**

(iii) It could also be asserted that a transfer of property, even when coupled with contemplation of, or an intention to make, an early entry to residential care, still does not by itself prove an intention to avoid liability for the fees. A transfer of assets could even be made with the intention that the enhanced proceeds from their better investment by trustees could provide sufficient income to pay for care if it ever becomes necessary.

(iv) Evidence of an ignorance of the rules can also be argued, as it has in income support cases, on the basis that there can be no avoidance intention if the alleged avoider does not know what he is avoiding **(see 4.16 - 4.18)**, but this argument was rejected in *Yule (No 2)* - **see 4.4** and **page 93** *infra*.

Local authority argument (2)

- the elderly person gave away the assets to one or more of his own children, thereby undermining his current assertion that the donation was not to protect his assets from a care fees assessment but to ensure the succession of his children to the assets, as the same result could have been achieved (ignoring the local authority's intervening claim!) by leaving the assets to the children in his Will.

(i) This argument appears to deny to those who may soon be faced with a liability for care fees the right to choose between an *inter vivos* transfer of property and *post mortem* testamentary arrangements, if the former is to be taken as cast iron proof of an avoidance intention. In fact the choice of an *inter vivos* arrangement says nothing by itself about the elderly person's purpose, intention, or knowledge.   It will usually be easier however to demonstrate a concern (unconnected with avoidance) that the assets be preserved for future generations if they have been transferred to a discretionary trust with appropriate directions. On the other hand a simple transfer to children or grandchildren who could easily dissipate the estate, or render it subject to the claims of their creditors would be less easy to defend.

(ii) The mere fact of disposal, no matter how unwise the choice of transferee, does not of itself prove an intention to avoid liability for care fees.

Local authority argument (3)

- the time elapsing between the donation and the entry to care was so short that there must have been an avoidance intention.

(i) Here again the local authority would be relying on a simple *non sequitur*. No court should uphold a case which is based on nothing more than a "must have been" argument. Early entry to care following a disposal says nothing, in the absence of other evidence, about the transferror's purpose, intention, or knowledge.

(ii) The defence will be stronger nevertheless if an emergency can be demonstrated (e.g. a sudden, unexpected, deterioration in health of the elderly person, or of someone who had undertaken to look after him at home) intervening between the disposal of assets and the entry to care. The length of the period between disposal and entry to care is however a relevant piece of evidence which has to be considered **(see 4.20.1)**.

Local authority argument (4)
- the person who made the transfer was of "great age" (79 years according to one local authority whose correspondence was seen by the author) so that the possibility of a requirement for residential care in the near future was "reasonably foreseeable".

(i) The logical effect of this argument is that no person of an age considered by their local authority to be "great" would be able to give away his assets without automatically being held to have done so with an avoidance purpose or intention. Nevertheless there is a strong flavour of this in *Yule (No 2)*. In England and Wales however where the case goes as far as insolvency proceedings precedent suggests that reasonable foreseeability of liability will have some bearing on proof of avoidance under **section 423** of the **Insolvency Act 1986 (see Ch 5)**. This (and the other preceding suggested replies to the local authority) assume of course that the assets were transferred prior to the issue of the local authority means assessment. It would be difficult to defend any disposal where it took place after intimation of the local authority's claim.

Dearth of Precedent
4.3   Only one case has been reported in which evidence of the transferror's purpose, intention, or knowledge at the time of transfer has been tested. *(Harcombe* **(see 1.24)** dealt not with a transferror's intention (as no transfers had been made) but with the intentions of the elderly person's son with regard to caring for her.) The case of *Yule v South Lanarkshire Council* (1998 SLT 480)* was a judicial review of the local authority's decision that the resident's house should be taken into account in her fees assessment although she had donated it to a granddaughter fifteen months prior to the entry to care. Initially that case was restricted to an examination of the local authority's powers to treat assets, transferred at any time, as notional capital, and it did no more than confirm what is clear law (that there is no time limit in **Regulation 25** of the **National Assistance (Assessment of Resources) Regulations 1992)**. **(For a fuller discussion of this case by the author see Scots Law Times of 1st May 1998 at page 105.)*

Mrs Yule's representatives argued that the only power available to the local authority is **section 21** of the **Health and Social Services and Social Security Adjudications Act 1983** (which deals with transfers within six months of the entry to care - **see 1.15**). They were not surprisingly unsuccessful as it has long been established that the local authority have the further power under **regulation 25** to treat as **notional capital** assets which have been disposed of at any time in the past. (This includes the six months prior to entry to care where it may be used by the local authority in a case where the fees are being paid by the resident, or on his behalf by relatives or a trust, so that there is no fees debt on which a claim under **section 21(1)(b)** of the **1983 Act** could be founded, and the local authority only require grounds to refuse a request for a contribution by them.) The court also confirmed the importance of the words "for the purpose of decreasing a possible liability to pay for care fees" in **regulation 25.** The case came to court again for a consideration of the facts (although these were ascertained from the exchange of correspondence between the lady's solicitors and the local authority (see *Yule v South Lanarkshire Council (No 2)* **at pages 92 - 95** *infra, and for a fuller discussion of this case by the author see also Scots Law Times, 18th June 1999 at page 175.*)

4.4   The facts considered by the court at the second hearing were as follows: a few months after the entry to care the local authority informed Mrs Yule that they were of the opinion that she had given away the house to avoid or reduce her future liability for care fees. The answer from her lawyers was to the effect that Mrs Yule had been in excellent health at the date of the gift, and that the reason for it was her particular fondness for the granddaughter. The local authority replied that such a result could have just as easily been achieved by leaving the house to the granddaughter in a Will. They added that, there being no other reason for the gift which they could accept, the reason for the gift must be the one they proposed, namely an attempt to protect the value of the house from inclusion in a care fees assessment.

4.5   The other evidence available was of a type which is likely to be common in such cases. The family claimed that at the date of the gift the lady was in good health and living independently and that her entry to care came about due to deterioration of health caused by an arm fracture subsequent to the date of the gift. Such an intervening incident, or the death or illness of a relative who at the time of disposal was expected to provide care in the home for the foreseeable future, should provide a good rebuttal of the local authority argument that the proximity of the date of disposal to the date of entry to care by itself proves an avoidance intention.

The local authority however claimed to have evidence from the Community Care assessment prepared just before the entry to care that the lady's son had reported a gradual deterioration in her health over the previous six or seven years.

4.6   The court decided in the favour of the local authority, and held that they were entitled to draw inferences from the fact that Mrs Yule "....was 78 when she disponed the fee of her dwellinghouse to her granddaughter. She retained the liferent of the house and continued to live in it until her accident. She could have achieved the same practical result by making a will in favour of her granddaughter. No clear explanation was provided to the respondents [the local authority] as to why the petitioner chose to give the house to Miss Yule by *inter vivos* transfer rather than by will..... The respondents were entitled to draw inferences from the information received by them.... It is a fact of life, which the respondents were entitled to take into account, that persons in their late seventies are increasingly likely to require nursing home accommodation. The avoidance of the requirement to meet the full cost of nursing home accommodation provided a motive for making the gift by *inter vivos* transfer of the property rather than by will. In so far as any other motive or explanation was provided to the respondents, they were entitled to reject it. In my view no satisfactory motive or explanation was in fact proffered."

Legal aid has been granted for an appeal to the Inner House of the Court of Session and it will be interesting to see if the appeal court upholds a theme which ran through much of the Outer House judgement to the effect that the local authority decision is purely administrative and can apparently therefore be made with little regard to the rules of natural justice which would apply to a judicial or semi-judicial decision.

In the meantime it should be noted that an *inter vivos* disposal of property to a discretionary trust rather than to a relative more effectively supports the argument that the disposal was made for the better administration of the property during the lifetime of the elderly person, something that a *post mortem* disposal obviously could never achieve. Nevertheless given the inference drawn in *Yule (No 2)* (see **page 93** *infra*) regarding the execution of a Power of Attorney, care must be taken to demonstrate that the setting up of the trust is intended to be a means of achieving better management of the elderly person's affairs, and more profitable investment of his assets, rather than to protect his assets against a care fees liability.

The Way to Court

4.7   In arguing a case of this type with the local authority it is important to have a clear understanding of the legal remedies available to the local authority and the limitations which these impose on them. The following situations can arise:-

4.7.1 Disposals within the six month period or after the entry to care

If the disputed disposal of assets took place **within the six month period**

Defend a Deprivation

prior to entry to care, or **after the entry to care**, the relevant statutory provision is **normally section 21** of the **1983 Act**. That provision applies to cash or any other asset which does not benefit from a disregard (see **1.19 - 1.25**). The first question will be whether the asset in dispute was actually owned by the resident. The next is whether such an owned asset has been the subject of a deprivation **(see 4.11 - 4.17)**. If there has been a deprivation the next question will be whether it was carried out "knowingly and with the intention of avoiding" charges for accommodation **(section 21(1)(b))**. The answers will depend on the facts. These will of course first be disputed in correspondence with the local authority. In the meantime the local authority will be bound to pay the care fees to the care provider and they cannot cease paying; nor can they evict the resident for nonpayment if the resident is living in a local authority home **(see 1.4)**. Once a local authority have made an assessment of need they must ensure that that need is met whether or not they manage to recover the cost **(section 12A** of the **Social Work (Scotland) Act 1968** and **section 47** of the **National Health Service and Community Care Act 1990)**.

If the dispute cannot be resolved in the resident's favour there will be two ways into court, one passive, the other active:-

(a) allow the debt to mount up until the local authority feel bound to take action under **section 21(1)(c)** of the **1983 Act** which imposes a liability on those to whom the assets were transferred within six months of, or after, entry to care to refund their value at the date of transfer to the local authority up to an amount equal to the care fees so far incurred. If this liability is disputed by the transferees the local authority will have to go to court using ordinary **debt recovery** procedures (as **section 21(1)(c)(ii)** of the **1983 Act** makes the transferee liable to **pay**, rather than hand back the transferred assets). The transferees, not the resident, will be the defenders, and they can lead in their defence any evidence which shows that the transfer to them by the resident was not done knowingly and with the intention of avoiding charges. As to the need for this intention to be "significant" if it sits alongside other intentions **see 4.21.1**. Both sides could be equally handicapped if the resident who made the transfer is unable to give evidence.

If the transferees are unsuccessful they will not only have to pay what is claimed but will also be liable for their own and the local authority's costs or expenses in the court action. Where the party to the action is a discretionary trust (e.g. as a transferee in circumstances where **section 21(1)(b)** could apply) the liability will fall on the trust funds and will not spill over to the trustees if they have acted in good faith and in accordance with the trust purposes.

(b) anticipate the local authority's debt recovery claim with an action for **judicial review** brought by the transferees of the property to have the local authority's decision (regarding the intention behind the asset transfer) declared invalid on the facts as agreed or proved. It is unlikely that such an action would be entertained in the name of the resident as he suffers no prejudice from the dispute between the local authority and the transferees as the local authority must continue to pay his care fees or provide care regardless of the outcome of that dispute. And here too if the transferee is a discretionary trust the expense of unsuccessful proceedings should fall on the trust funds.

4.7.2 Disposals more than six months prior to entry to care

Even if the disputed disposal of assets took place within six months prior to, or after, entry to care the local authority may choose to rely on **regulation 25** of the **1992 Regulations** rather than **section 21** of the **1983 Act (see 4.3 above)** but where the disposal took place **more than six months** prior to entry to care this provision will be the only one directly available to them. It enables the local authority to calculate the resident's contribution to the care fees with reference not only to capital which the resident still possesses but also the value of assets which he has disposed of "for the purpose of decreasing the amount that he may be liable to pay for his accommodation" i.e. **notional capital**. The local authority's liability to the care provider will still persist and they cannot cease to pay, or cease to provide the accommodation themselves if the resident is in a local authority home, even if the resident or his representatives refuse to accept that the transferred assets should be treated as notional capital and refuse to make a contribution based on them.

Here again there will be two ways into court but in both it is the resident who will be the party opposing or challenging the local authority as the case will be about recovering the debt (which only the resident can run up) rather than making transferrees pay (as **section 21(1)(c)(ii)** of the **1983 Act** does not apply to disposals made more than six months before entry to care):-

(a) the resident can refuse to pay the assessment in so far as it is based on the inclusion of the notional capital so that once the debt has mounted up the local authority will have to go to court in a **debt recovery** action under **section 22(1)** of the **1948 Act**. It is in the defence to these proceedings that the resident, through his representatives, will lead evidence to demonstrate that the transfer was made for a purpose other than that caught by **regulation 25. The local authority (with an eye to *Yule (No2)*) may however plead that their decision itself founds the debt recovery action and that while it remains in place (i.e. not successfully challenged in judicial review) no evidence can be heard in the debt recovery action to challenge its soundness.** If the resident is unsuccessful in his defence an order will be made against him for the amount claimed plus the local authority's costs or expenses in the action. As **regulation 25** provides no power

Defend a Deprivation

comparable to that provided by **section 21** of the **1983 Act** they will not be able to recover these, or the principle sum, out of the transferred assets, nor do they have any power to retrieve these assets from the transferees other than by starting insolvency proceedings against the resident in which case they may be met with various defences under insolvency legislation (see **Ch 5**).

(b) the resident can anticipate the local authority's debt recovery action by himself seeking a **judicial review** of the local authority's decision to treat the transferred assets as notional capital. If he is unsuccessful the local authority will be able to recover any costs or expenses awarded against him only out of such capital as he retains or income he receives. As the income will already be defraying the care fees so far as it can there will be no advantage to the local authority in diverting it to payment of their court costs or expenses. Clearly the relatives of the resident and transferees of his property (including discretionary trusts) are in a better position where **regulation 25** applies as with all proceedings having to be taken against or initiated by the resident himself, no liability falls on relatives or transferees.

4.8 There appears to be no advantage in the resident or the transferees initiating court action in disputes arising out of either **section 21** or **regulation 25**. They can do so only by judicial review which is a process better suited to testing the powers of a decision-making body than assessing the evidence on which the decision is based. (Judicial review should not be used as a fact finding process - *R v Chief Constable for Warwickshire ex parte F*, The Times, 26th November 1997, and *Reid v Secretary of State for Scotland* H.L.(Sc) [1999] 2 WLR 28 at page 54). Post *Yule* any questions there may have been about the local authority's powers regarding notional capital have been resolved in their favour, so that it is the facts rather than the law which will be the cause of any dispute now. The lower courts (Sheriff, in **Scotland**, and County, in **England and Wales**) in which the local authorities will raise their actions for recovery of unpaid care fees are well suited to hearing the evidence of innocent intention which a resident and his relatives will want to offer in defence (unless the court accepts a local authority argument that their decision having been made, and not challenged in judicial review, it cannot then be challenged in the debt recovery proceedings).

The debt action can be brought only by the local authority which is an advantage to the resident whose knowledge or intention are disputed as the local authority, for reasons of lethargy or lack of confidence in the outcome, may well delay or never bring the case to court. That delay will also give the relatives more time to assess how far the resident's income falls short of the care fees so as to make a decision whether or not to make up the shortfall themselves rather than put the resident's estate, or transferred assets (if **section 21** applies), at risk of diminution in a court case.

4.9 Regardless of whether court proceedings are likely to result in any personal liability the resident's relatives may prefer to avoid the effort and worry which these will demand especially at a time when they are already burdened by concern for the resident, a loved one whose declining health and consequent entry to residential care has caused the dispute. At this stage a careful calculation should be made of all the resident's actual and potential income and an attempt made to maximise it. For example, if attendance allowance is not being paid only because the residential care home is owned or managed by the local authority (see **2.4**) consideration should be given to a move to a place which is not so owned or managed. The relatives will also know by this time what the resident's care fees will be each year. If the difference between the amount required and the amount which can be paid out of the resident's income from all sources, is small enough for the relatives to bear they may find it advantageous to make this up themselves rather than engage in a lengthy dispute with the local authority especially if the outcome could result in the loss of a substantial proportion of the resident's estate. An obvious case in which relatives might prefer to pay would be one in which the resident's house had been donated to a son or daughter so that they no longer have to pay a mortgage. A contribution to the care fees up to an amount equal to what they would have paid for a mortgage may be preferable to a hazardous litigation.

There is also a difficult choice to be made if the resident's residual estate is small or non-existent (having been mostly transferred and now forming the notional capital which gives rise to the dispute). If the local authority base an assessment on the notional capital and raise a debt recovery action against the resident why bother to defend it when there are no assets out of which the local authority can recover either the principal sum or the cost of the action no matter how technically successful they may be in court? This would be an attractive strategy if insolvency procedures were not also available to the local authority. However faced with the choice of establishing innocent intention sooner in debt recovery proceedings rather than later in insolvency proceedings many people may prefer to offer no defence in the debt recovery action and hope that the insolvency proceedings, for one reason or another, never happen.

Complaints Procedure
4.10 The local authority complaints procedure has already been referred to at **1.10**. It is unlikely to appeal to anyone in dispute with a local authority regarding the intention behind a disposal of assets where liability for care fees is in question. The effectiveness and impartiality of the procedure vary from one authority to another and depend very much on the calibre of the local authority official, known as the "designated officer", who is supposed to ensure not only that complaints are dealt with in compliance with the statutory time limits, but also that there is genuine commitment to the process.

The procedure starts off with an **"informal" stage** during which an attempt is made to resolve the complaint. There is no statutory limit on how long this may last although individual authorities may prescribe "best practice" time limits. It is followed by the **formal stage** in which the complaint will normally have to be put forward in writing and the social services department given a chance to reply. Time limits are applied at this stage but not always observed. There should then be an investigation of the complaint, but although the principles of natural justice will normally be applied so that the investigation is carried out by officials not directly involved with the subject matter of the complaint they will usually be employed by the local authority against whom the complaint is being made.

The local authority consider a report on the investigation and then produce their decision which may or may not modify the decision complained of. There is no requirement for the investigator's report to be made available to the complainer, but if he is dissatisfied with the decision and proceeds to the **third stage** when the complaint will be heard by a panel of three persons the report will have to be made available so that he can argue his case properly.

Of the three persons on the panel only one need be "independent". If of the other two one is an official and the other a councillor of the authority the complainer's trust in the independence of the procedure may be somewhat diminished. The panel does act as a fact finding body and could therefore in theory be well adapted to resolving a dispute about an avoidance intention but where a question of law arises, e.g. the proper interpretation of "for the purpose of" in **regulation 25** or "knowingly" in **section 21** the panel is not even qualified to make a pronouncement and will normally base its recommendations on the local authority's interpretation of the law as relayed to them by the local authority's solicitor. The complainer will have gone through a tedious process to achieve nothing.

Even if after a consideration of the facts the panel make a recommendation in favour of the complainer the local authority are not bound to act on it, though they do have to give a well reasoned argument for not acting if they are not to risk a challenge in court. For many people therefore it will be preferable to let the fees debt mount up, or leave the transferred property with the transferees, and let the local authority go to court in debt recovery procedures, where their position can be challenged before an impartial bench. In any case the courts have now made it clear that judicial review and not the complaints procedure is the appropriate procedure where the dispute concerns the local authority's legal obligations (*R v Gloucestershire CC, ex p Radar* (1998) 1 C. C. L Rep. 476).

Deprivations

4.11   In disputes regarding residential care fees assessments the first important question is whether there has or has not been a deprivation. A resident will not normally want to claim that he has not deprived himself of assets because if he has failed to do so the local authority can then definitely take them into account in his care fees assessment. For example if a resident has failed to properly deprive himself of any house or land which he possesses the local authority can not only take it into account in calculating the care fees assessment they can also use sections **22 or 23** of the **Health and Social Social Services and Social Security Adjudications Act 1983** to impose a charge on the property so that when it is sold they can recoup any accumulated fees debt out of the proceeds.

4.12   Ideally therefore what a resident will want to prove is that there has been an effective deprivation of property but that the intention behind the deprivation is not caught (depending on the time it took place) either by **section 21** of the **1983 Act** or **regulation 25 of the 1992 Regulations**. The best place to find arguments for or against a deprivation is in the Social Security Commissioners' income support archive. There the claimant has an interest to prove that he either does not own assets above a certain amount or that he has deprived himself of them without any significant intention of doing so in order to qualify for income support. Under the care fees regime the resident wants to prove that he has deprived himself of assets with no intention of avoiding liability for care fees. If he succeeds in that he will have all or part of his care fees paid by the local authority, and the value of his transferred property cannot be reclaimed from transferees, or made the subject of a charge (under the **1983 Act**), or treated as notional capital (under the **1992 Regulations).** The income support claimant who fails to prove a deprivation simply receives no benefit. A resident in care however who fails to prove an innocent disposal of his house could lose it to the local authority.

4.13   In attempting to prove a deprivation the first thing the local authority have to allege is **ownership prior to disposal** (just as a prosecutor has to produce an owner before he can prove theft) as no-one can deprive himself of ownership of an item which he has borrowed, or hired, or held only on trust. If the local authority are unable to do this they will never be able to impose any liability on alleged transferees under **section 21** or treat the value of the allegedly transferred assets as notional capital under **regulation 25**. They will be able to search any public register, such as property or company registers, for evidence of ownership and transfers, but they can only ask for bank statements or access to bank accounts, having, unlike the taxman, no powers (outwith those which can be granted in the course of litigation) to search for, or demand production of, private documents. However when the assessment of means is made the process cannot progress without completion of the assessment form. Any false claims or declarations made in the form could be the basis for a charge of fraud brought against the signatory.

Defend a Deprivation

4.14　In many cases if there is any defence to an allegation of ownership and subsequent deprivation it will be obvious enough, for example, that the house was originally disponed to a person other than the one in care, and has never been owned by him, or it has always been held in trust for someone else. Production of the title deeds in such simple cases will put an end to that part of the local authority's claim. Evidence of a mortgage secured over the property could have virtually the same effect as the part of the value covered by the secured loan cannot be taken into account. The more difficult case is the one in which some form of unwritten or resultant trust arrangement has to be proved (see **1.29 - 1.32.1**).

4.15　The second thing to be alleged by the local authority is that the resident has indeed **deprived** himself of the asset for less than its market value. The simple case is the one where the resident has given an asset away and received nothing in return. The title deeds will provide the evidence where the asset was a house or land. Less obvious are the cases where money is converted into something else which is either less valuable (purchase of an expensive car for example which will be worth much less than its purchase price as soon as it is driven out of the showroom), or the purchase of an asset which is disregarded under the regulations **(see 1.19 - 1.25)**. Examples of the latter would be certain personal possessions, or a life insurance policy. The general theme is that where a readily marketable asset such as a house has been given away, or cash has been used to purchase an item which is worth less than the price paid for it, or is an item which is to be treated as disregarded for assessment purposes, there has been a deprivation (**see 4.19.1**)

The value of the asset given away, or converted to something else, will be subject to the provisions of **section 21** of the **1983 Act** or will be treated as notional capital under **regulation 25**. One Social Security Commissioner's decision, CIS/494/1990, suggests that where a conversion has taken place the notional capital is only the difference between the purchase price and the current value of the item purchased, with the acquired item being assessed as actual capital.

The preferred interpretation however is that the handing over of the purchase price is the deprivation so that it is that amount which is treated as notional capital. That avoids the awkward problem of assessing the ever declining value of the purchase. Some acquired items however may increase in value so that one could foresee a local authority referring to this otherwise aberrant decision to argue that the item should be treated as actual capital with the deprivation made to acquire it ignored. The reported decision, R(SB) 40/85, (see **4.19.1**) however can be used to controvert this line of argument.

4.16　The most difficult question for both parties is proof of the **intention** behind the donation or purchase. **Section 21** of the **1983 Act** uses the words "knowingly

Defend a Deprivation

and with the intention of avoiding charges" and **regulation 25** uses the words "for the purpose of decreasing the amount that he may be liable to pay". Although the words are quite different the difference is superficial: "purpose" must include both knowledge and intention if it is to retain its proper meaning. The evidence in cases under either provision should therefore be directed to the same end as far as the resident is concerned. He either did not know that the deprivation would result in an avoidance of charges or he had no intention of avoiding them.

As regulation 51 of the Income Support (General) Regulations uses the words "for the purpose of securing entitlement" Commissioners' decisions may provide a useful guide to the proper assessment of facts regarding knowledge and intention in care fees cases. According to some of these ignorance of the law, contrary to the general expectation, can be an excuse. It is not enough that an income support claimant ought to have been aware of the deprivation rules. He has to be actually aware of them before an intention to avoid them can be attributed to him. However his background and intellectual capacity will be taken into account together with the likelihood that he has received advice from friends or professional advisers. An ignorance-of-the-law defence is less likely to be successful in cases under the care fees regime as the asset most often in dispute is the house, the disposal of which will normally require professional advice. It would be difficult in such cases where the transferror is an elderly person to convince a court that the assessment rules were not mentioned at the time of the transaction.

4.17 However as receipt of income support for many years will not by itself prove knowledge of the rules (Social Security Commissioner's decision R(SB)12/91) the long term resident who has a windfall and gives it away may not be deemed to do so in full knowledge of the rules even if he is still capable of managing his own affairs. Educational background and occupation (e.g. as a social security official) will however be material evidence of a knowledge of the rules (R(SB) 12/91 at paragraph 15).

4.18 However even if a knowledge of the rules has to be conceded that in itself will not prove an avoidance intention. And according to the income support precedents even if knowledge is admitted or proved such an intention occurring among others would have to be the significant intention for an avoidance one to be proved (**see 4.21.1**). It would appear therefore that assets could be given away to ensure their better management for the benefit of the existing and succeeding generations (the typical discretionary trust arrangement) and the donor could still admit to an awareness that an **incidental** effect would be to remove the assets from any care fees assessment which may take place in the future.

Social Security Commissioners' Decisions

4.19 A glance at any welfare rights hand book will reveal numerous Social Security

Defend a Deprivation

Commissioners decisions on income support and supplementary benefit which appear to be relevant to the assessment of resources for residential care. Superficial acquaintance alone may suggest that many of them could be used by a local authority to support their arguments set out at **4.2** above. A closer examination however suggests that they do not so much lay down hard and fast interpretations of "for the purpose of" as emphasise that each case turns on its own facts. They also set out "rules" to be followed in such cases for the gathering of facts and their relevance to the legal interpretation.

For example the leading decision is R(SB)40/85, a supplementary benefit case, still followed for income support questions, and never challenged in the courts. (This and other Commissioners' decisions on supplementary benefit may also be useful for cases where it is to be argued that although the existence of notional capital is admitted or proved the local authority should nevertheless exercise their discretion not to take it into account, for they are not bound to do so. The supplementary benefit regulations gave the adjudication officer a **discretion** (later withdrawn in subsequent income support legislation) whether or not to treat a resource as notional capital if the claimant was proved to have deprived himself of it with the requisite intention. That same discretionary element is still found in the current local authority care fees regime.)

4.19.1 Social Security Commissioner's Decision (R(SB)40/85

(1) For the transferred asset to be treated as notional capital three things have to be proved: "(1) .... the claimant ....has deprived himself of a resource; (2)....he has done so for the purpose of securing supplementary benefit or increasing the amount of such benefit [*cf.* decreasing the amount that he may be liable to pay for his accommodation] and (3) ... it is appropriate to exercise the discretionary power of treating the resource as still possessed by the claimant [*cf.* resident].." (paragraph 4).

(2) The meaning of "deprive": "....it does not change its meaning by reference to the consequences of deprivation. It is .... perfectly proper ... to conclude that a person has deprived himself of a resource if as the result of his own act he ceases to possess that resource whether or not he becomes possessed of some other resource in its place. He may thus be held to have deprived himself of a resource if he gives it away, if he uses it up in living frugally or prodigally, or to pay for a holiday or in any other manner that leaves no resource at the end of the day; or if he uses it to purchase a resource of equal value which will retain its value; or which will rapidly depreciate or which will fall to be disregarded for purposes of supplementary benefit [*cf.* assessment]" (paragraph 8).

(3) The purpose of the deprivation: "It is not normally possible to ascertain a person's purpose from direct evidence....... Ordinarily the purpose is a matter of inference from primary facts found. The present case is one where there are facts which if they stood alone might lead to the legitimate conclusion that the claimant had deprived himself of cash resources for the purpose of securing, or increasing the amount of, supplementary benefit [*cf.*

decreasing the amount that he may be liable to pay for his accommodation]. But there are other facts which may be taken as pointing the other way." There then follow directions to the tribunal to which the case is to be remitted. These should be adopted by any local authority making an assessment decision: "Facts should be included whether they tell for or against the conclusion reached and some indications should be given of those to which weight has been attached. ...The claimant has tendered reasons for various items of expenditure, such as his wife's state of health, and the fact that he had booked the holiday before he was made redundant. Findings are essential on these matters. ....some question has been raised as to the state of the claimant's knowledge of the capital limits and a finding will be necessary..... It is certainly possible for a person without knowledge of the details ..... to have the purpose of depriving himself of resources with a view to securing, or increasing the amount of, supplementary benefit [*cf.* decreasing the amount he may be liable to pay for his accommodation.]" (paragraph 9).

(4) **"significant operative purpose"**: "It is not necessary that the purpose of securing, or increasing the amount of, supplementary benefit [*cf.* decreasing liability for care fees] shall be the sole purpose, though it must be a significant operative purpose. ....if the evidence showed that the transaction had had the effect of securing this, ... and that this was the foreseeable consequence of it and there was nothing more, a tribunal could legitimately conclude that the person's purpose was to secure supplementary benefit [cf. decreased liability]. But there may well be other evidence e.g. *[explaining the reason for spending resources on a carpet, which being a personal possession is disregarded in an assessment of assets]* that the existing floor covering was worn out, or that a member of the assessment unit [*cf.* household] was allergic to dust to an extent that wall to wall carpeting was medically advisable." (paragraph 10).

4.20   R(SB) 40/85 followed and built on an earlier Commissioner's Decision, R(SB) 38/85.

4.20.1 Social Security Commissioner's Decision R(SB) 38/85

Paragraph 18 of this decision deals with the **standard of proof** and the **onus of proving**: "Once it has been shown that a member of the assessment unit has recently received, or otherwise been the owner of, a capital resource .... the onus of proving, on a balance of probability, that he no longer has that resource rests on *the claimant,* since it is for him to establish title to supplementary benefit....... The claimant says that he expended this sum ..... in repaying loans. It is for him to prove that this is so. Failing a satisfactory account of the way in which the money has been disposed of, it will be open to the tribunal, and a natural conclusion, to find that the claimant still has, in some form or other, that resource and consequently to conclude that his actual resources are above the prescribed limit."

When this advice is applied to a assessment of care fees liability there can be no cavil with the suggestion that the standard of proof should, as in all civil

Defend a Deprivation

cases, rest on the balance of probabilities. With regard to the onus of proof however it could be argued that it is for the local authority to prove liability. Like the DSS they have to allege a deprivation of assets but they have to couple this with their own entitlement to a contribution by the resident towards the care fees which the needs assessment has informed them to be necessary. A DSS claimant seeks to establish or increase his entitlement to benefit whereas a resident in residential care seeks to deny or reduce his liability care fees, but it is the local authority which claims entitlement to the resident's assets. This decision also provides at paragraph 25 a useful summary of the way a decision maker should approach a deprivation issue:

> "Findings should be made on the following:-
>
> **(1) On how the deprivation actually occurred.** While not accepting that there is any actual presumption that a gift of a resource should be taken to be for the purpose of obtaining supplementary benefit or that payment for a service (e.g. a surgical operation) should be taken to have no such object, these are clearly material facts. Findings as to what actually happened, with dates and amounts are clearly material.
>
> **(2) The personal circumstances of the claimant.** For example, his age, state of health, and his future employment prospects may affect the conclusion reached as to the claimant's objects in repaying loans, or otherwise disposing of his resources, and the way in which the adjudicating authority's discretion is exercised. He may have urgent requirements which can only be met out of his capital and in no other way.
>
> **(2) The reason why the claimant acted in the way that he did,** in depriving himself of the resource in question. For example, where a loan is repaid, was there any pressure being applied to repay? Where a gift is made, why was it made at that time?
>
> **(2) The dates and period over which the disposal occurred.** The nearness, or distance, from the date of claim has obvious relevance."

4.21   Further refinements of the intention doctrine are found in R(SB) 9/91.

4.21.1 Social Security Commissioner's Decision R(SB) 9/91

Paragraph 8 draws a useful distinction between **consequence** and **intention**: "I do not think that it was enough for the tribunal merely to say that "the natural *consequence*.... of the gift was to secure an allowance. A positive *intention* to secure benefit has to be shown." When applied to the local authority care fees regime this argument gains strength from the fact that **section 21** of the **1983 Act** and **regulation 25** of the **1992 Regulations** contain requirements as to knowledge and intention, or purpose.

Paragraphs 10 and 11 are instructive for those who have made or are contemplating a **gift of the house to children.** An Affidavit was lodged on behalf of the applicant which contained the following declaration: "I know very little about any ......rules. When I decided to give my old home .... to my 2 daughters the only thought in my mind was that the house was no longer any good to me and that since I intended to leave the house to my two daughters in my Will I wished to give it to them in my lifetime. This was the only reason for the Deed of Gift being made in my lifetime." An attendance note made by the applicant's solicitor also confirmed that he had put the question of intention to the applicant and she had made it clear that her sole concern was to benefit the two daughters.

The Commissioner however considered the evidence in the Affidavit to be of limited value: "It clearly shows that the claimant intended to make a *gift* of the property, and did not wish to retain any beneficial interest by way of a resulting trust...... But it does not show why she wanted the property to pass to her daughters *at that particular time*. To say that "the house was no longer any good to me" - she intended to go into a nursing home after she left hospital and in fact moved there within three weeks - does not resolve the far more important question, ..., why the *proceeds of sale* of the house were no longer of any use to her. If a person decides he or she has no longer any need for his or her present home, the normal reaction is to sell it and take the proceeds of sale. ....in giving away the house, the claimant also gave away its realisable value, and no explanation appears in the affidavit as to why the claimant adopted this course. To say that the property was left to the two daughters in the claimant's Will is no explanation as to why she decided to donate it in her lifetime. This was not the case of a rich lady who could afford to give away her home , and still have ample resources to live on." - (paragraph 11).

Although at first glance R(SB) 9/91 may be depressing news for those who have given away assets in similar circumstances it is rather less so for those who choose a discretionary trust as the destination. The *"at that particular time"* argument can be answered to the effect that old age and frailty were making the personal maintenance and administration of the property increasingly burdensome, so that a donation to trustees was an obvious solution to the problem. The question of how the donor is to live and maintain himself is also answered if he is a beneficiary under the trust. Trustees (of whom the donor may be one) in proper exercise of their discretion would allow the donor to live on in the house (or one more suited to his needs purchased with its proceeds) and to receive at their discretion so much of the trust income as they deemed appropriate. A similar expectation cannot be relied on where the assets are donated to relatives.

If however the condition of the donor was such that he knew at the time of donation that he was about to go into residential care it would be difficult to argue the need for a trust to look after the house as it would normally be sold after the entry to care. It could nevertheless be argued that there was a possibility of the donor finding residential care uncongenial so that it was advisable to keep the house available in the meantime, and that it along

Defend a Deprivation

with the other assets would be better looked after by trustees. It might also be argued that the impending need for care was itself a clear indicator that the estate would require competent management by trustees.

R(SB) 9/91 deals also with the questions of **predominant motive** and **significant operative purpose**. At paragraph 14 the Commissioner says: "It must be borne in mind that securing supplementary benefit need not be the *predominant* motive underlying the relevant transaction. As was said in R(SB) 38/85 at paragraph 22:- "Suppose a claimant on supplementary benefit inherits a large sum of money and proceeds to gamble with it and incur losses. Someone warns him that if he continues in this way he will be back on supplementary benefit and he replies 'if I lose, that is my idea'. His predominant purposes in gambling with the money would obviously be to win at gambling. But it would be open to the adjudicating authority to decide on these facts that another purpose was to obtain supplementary benefit." In the present case the predominant motive was doubtless to advance the claimant's children. But a **significant operative purpose** was also to obtain supplementary benefit in the same exercise. In other words the claimant's intention was to kill two birds with one stone, to accelerate the daughters' inheritance and at the same time to claim supplementary benefit. There were two coordinate purposes.

4.22 In an unreported income support case, CIS/242/1993, a different result was obtained by the claimant, and it provides a useful reminder that such cases are to be decided on their facts. No adminicle of evidence which might persuade a court that the intention behind a disposal was "innocent" should be ignored.

4.22.1 Social Security Commissioner's Decision CIS/242/1993

In his conclusion at paragraph 13 the Commissioner states: "..... there was a deprivation by the claimant ..... of her share in the proceeds of sale .... but equally I conclude that by so depriving herself of that share she did not do so "for the purpose of securing entitlement to income support".....My ultimate conclusion is that the the claimant's son is correct when he submits ..... as follows, "[My late mother's] purpose of relinquishing her share in the sale of proceeds in her son's favour was not that of securing entitlement to Income Support or increasing the amount of that benefit, but was in fact in recognition of some 15 years he had cared for her following her husband's death and to enable her son to purchase a suitable property for himself and his future wife". I conclude ..... that this is not the case of an attempt by a relation of an elderly person to obtain the elderly person's capital and cast that person on to the income support fund,....... it is clear to me from the papers that he had in fact been involved in considerable work and anxiety in looking after his late mother and is to be commended for the way in which it is clear that he did so. I do not consider it <u>unrealistic on the facts of this case</u> to regard the ultimate relinquishment of the share in the proceeds of sale ..... as being referable to gratitude to the son for this." This is clear support for the **"recompense argument"** suggested at **paragraphs 5.11 - 5.13 below.**

56

5

Avoid Insolvency Proceedings

As the local authorities become increasingly desperate for cash they may use insolvency law to get beyond the six month time limit imposed by section 21 of the 1983 Act and attack transfers which took place up to five years or even longer before the move into residential care.

5.2 What local authorities may do is accept the person into residential care, treat as notional capital assets which have been transferred on a date more than six months prior to entry to care (and therefore not caught by **section 21** of the **1983 Act**), make the appropriate assessment, let the bills mount up for some time and then **render the resident bankrupt.** In the subsequent bankruptcy proceedings the authority would argue that the disposal to relatives, or a trust, is a disposal of a kind caught by insolvency laws designed to prevent unfair treatment of creditors. Such transactions can be cut down retrospectively so that those who received the assets have to hand them back or account for their value. Fortunately this suggestion would turn out in most cases to be no more than a bluff or an unscrupulous attempt to frighten people off from trying to arrange their affairs in such a way as to minimise their liability. So far local authorities have only threatened insolvency proceedings and none, as far as can be ascertained, have had the confidence actually to put a case in court.

The Solvency Defence

5.3 The problem for local authorities in trying to take advantage of insolvency laws (so far as they relate to **transactions at an undervalue in England and Wales** and **gratuitous alienations in Scotland**) lies in the fact that a disposal by a bankrupt in the **five** year period prior to commencement of bankruptcy proceedings cannot be cut down if at any time after the disposal the bankrupt was solvent (under the exception in **England and Wales** that if the transaction took place in the **two** year period prior to the commencement of the bankruptcy proceedings the solvency defence is excluded (**section 341(2)** of the **Insolvency Act 1986**)). Most ordinary elderly persons who give away their houses and other assets to relatives or a trust will not become insolvent in doing so. They will continue to have some income such as

Avoid Insolvency Proceedings

their retirement pension and will never be in the position of not being able to pay for their daily needs as they arise. They are in fact likely to be solvent for most of the period between disposal and beyond entry into residential care prior to the attempt by the local authority to bankrupt them.

5.4 Section 341(3)(b) of the **Insolvency Act 1986** (which applies in **England and Wales**) does provide that an individual is to be regarded as insolvent if at the **relevant time** "the value of his assets is less than the amount of his liabilities, taking into account his contingent and prospective liabilities". Therein lies the germ of an argument for the local authorities that anyone who disposes of property within the five year period prior to going into residential care, and who is aware of the general possibility that faces everybody, that some day he *may* require residential care, has a *prospective* liability for those fees.

The contrary argument is that an awareness that residential care fees may some day have to be incurred, if one lives long enough, and the need arises, is not by itself a prospective liability in the way intended by the statute, especially if it can be demonstrated that there was no avoidance intention associated with the disposal, and that there was at the time no specific indication (as opposed to a vague possibility dependent on the cards life deals) that residential care would ever be required. The purpose of insolvency legislation is to protect creditors and investors who deal with enterprises, which have been set up to make a profit, and whose proprietors arrange their affairs and assets in a way which will disadvantage such creditors and investors as are attracted to deal with them. The elderly person who eventually falls into ill-health so as to require residential care, and the local authority who are bound by statute to meet his needs, albeit entitled to collect recompense for doing so, are rather different, both in their nature and their relationship, from business entrepreneurs and their customers.

5.5 In **Scotland** the comparable provisions of the **Bankruptcy (Scotland) Act 1985 (sections 34** and **36)** say nothing explicitly about *prospective* liabilities, and there is no doubt that solvency intervening between the transaction by which assets are disposed of and the date of sequestration prevents the transaction from being cut down. (The **Scottish** common law on bankruptcy allows such transactions up to twenty years old to be examined but here again, as under the statute, intervening solvency will protect the transaction from reduction.)

Innocent Intention Essential

5.6 The other area of insolvency law in **England and Wales** which could be attractive to local authorities seeking to reduce transfers of assets is that dealing with **transactions defrauding creditors** where assets have been transferred as a gift or at an undervalue. These are dealt with at sections

Avoid Insolvency Proceedings

423 and 424 of the **Insolvency Act 1986**. Such transactions can be cut down however only if the court can be satisfied that they were entered into with the **intention** of putting assets beyond the reach of the person or body who is challenging the transactions (note the all-encompassing nature of **section 424(1)(c)**), or of otherwise prejudicing their interests in relation to any claim they were making or **may make in the future**.

5.7 **Section 423** was applied in the recent case of *Midland Bank PLC v Wyatt [1997]* 1 BCLC 242. The defendant had in 1981 executed a legal charge in favour of the bank on a house purchased jointly with his wife to provide security for a house mortgage loan and overdraft on their joint current account. In 1987 the defendant entered into a declaration of trust donating his interest in the house to his wife and two daughters. The bank's right to enforce the charging order in 1991 was upheld by the court which accepted the bank's contention that the declaration of trust in favour of the wife and family had been a sham transaction and was in breach of **section 423**. It held that the defendant had no intention of disposing of his interest to benefit his family, and that the true reason for the declaration of trust was to guard against the uncertain risks associated with a new business which he was at that time contemplating. What mattered was the intention or purpose underlying the transaction. In the court's opinion the defendant's true intention was to put his interest in the house out of the reach of any future creditors who might be entitled to make a claim on it.

5.7.1 If however an elderly person is concerned that on his death his estate will pass to offspring who may squander it, and therefore transfers it during his lifetime to a discretionary trust in which his children are potential beneficiaries, the childrens' creditors will not be able to use **section 423** against the elderly donor as he is not liable for the childrens' debts. Nor can the childrens' creditors go against the discretionary trust as it has a legal personality of its own, separate from that of the children. And the local authority will not be able to use the provision against the elderly person for a care fees assessment if all the evidence points to a transfer to the trust to protect the estate not from such an assessment but rather from dissipation by those who would otherwise succeed directly to it. Nor need the offspring be depicted as Regency rakes: many young people with a mortgage, and job insecurity are vulnerable to financial mishaps so that the good sense of putting their inheritance into a trust can be easily demonstrated thus seeing off any challenge by a local authority regarding the "true" intention.

5.8 In **Scotland** the common law recognises the concept of the **fraudulent preference** but only in the context of a person who is already insolvent engaging in transactions designed to benefit one or more creditors in preference to others. Where a transaction is challenged as an **unfair preference** using the **statutory** provisions the challenger need prove only that the transaction took place less than six months before the date of sequestration - a period already provided for in the context of residential care fees by section **21(1)(b)(i)** of the **Health and Social Services and Social Security Adjudications Act 1983**. (Scots therefore may gain no advantage in taking on the difficult task provided for in that section (where a transfer of property took place **within** the six months prior to entry to care) of proving that they did not "knowingly and with the intention of avoiding charges" dispose of their property, as the local authority could challenge any transfer during that period **regardless of intention** if the circumstances of the case were such that the unfair preference provisions of Scottish bankruptcy legislation could be invoked.)

5.9   If such a challenge is based on **Scottish common law** (because longer than six months have elapsed since the date of the transaction) the challenger has to prove that the debtor was absolutely insolvent at the time of the transaction or as a consequence of it and is also absolutely insolvent at the time of the challenge, an unlikely situation where an elderly person has made a prudent and carefully considered transfer of assets.

5.10 It is essential therefore in the bankruptcy context, particularly in **England and Wales**, that **no evidence by word or deed** either at the time of the transaction or at any date in the future, could indicate that the purpose of the transaction is to avoid liability for payment of residential care fees. Indeed if assets are being transferred to a discretionary trust some other **positive purpose** should be stated such as "the better management and preservation of the family estate" or "to make better provision for one's children" (to guard against their likely tendency to dissipate their inheritance). And care should be taken to ensure that the person disposing of assets does not thereby render himself insolvent.

The Recompense Argument

5.11 One argument which could be deployed, if there are bankruptcy proceedings (or even if there are not), and which will certainly take up some time, as it has not yet been tested in the courts, is that there can be no element of undervaluation or gratuitousness where the assets of a person who has received care at home are transferred to the person who provided it. Can they not wholly or partly be regarded as **proper recompense** for services rendered? For the seeds of this argument, which is yet to be developed in the residential care field, refer to *Re Kumar (a bankrupt), ex parte Lewis v Kumar and another* [1993]2 AER 700 and authorities discussed there. For support from a Social Security Commissioner, albeit in a decision which he describes as turning on its own facts, see CIS/242/1993 referred to at **4.22** above.

5.12 However if the recompense argument were to succeed it would be applicable only to cases where the assets had been transferred to a person who provided care. It would not normally succeed where assets have been transferred to some other person or to a trust, but a transfer to a trust could possibly work where the carer to be recompensed is made a sole beneficiary of the trust and the trust purpose is stated as being "to recompense X for caring services rendered". A further difficulty is that if care fees have already been incurred and not paid the local authority will be in competition for recompense out of the resident's assets: a transfer to a previous carer even if ostensibly for services rendered could be regarded under the insolvency legislation as an attempt to disadvantage other creditors. As these are uncharted waters this device should be considered only as an additional fall back position or where entry to care is imminent and no other escape route is available.

5.13 Nevertheless where care has been or is being provided in the home by a friend or relative to whom the assets are intended to pass it would always be advisable to draw up an informal record of the number of hours spent on caring, preceded by an exchange of letters indicating that the carer will be recompensed. There is no reason why the proper rate of recompense for such caring should not equate to that charged by nursing agencies. On these terms the value of care provided by a relative could soon amount to the value of a house, and would at least provide a sound factual and evidential basis for challenging the local authority's claim on the assets in respect of care fees still to be incurred. (If Invalid Care Allowance has been claimed the DSS will have records showing that 35 hours or more per week have been spent in caring).

Delay Inadvisable

5.14 It will be obvious from what is discussed above and in **Chapter 4** that, although a disposal of assets can safely be made at any time if the requisite non-avoidance intention can be demonstrated (and regardless of whether the local authority challenge is based on local authority welfare law or insolvency law), the disposal should take place as long as possible before the entry into residential care as the more time that has elapsed the less likely the local authority will be able to find, or willing to seek, evidence that the disposal was made with the intention of avoiding payment of residential care fees.

6

Render Unto Caesar*

It is never possible to escape the taxman. Transfer of personal assets, and the income from them, to a trust reduces or eliminates the personal burden but they will continue to be subject to taxation in the hands of the trustees.

Income Tax

6.2 The rate of **Income Tax** applicable to discretionary trusts remains unchanged at 34% although the basic rate of personal income tax for 1999/2000 is only 23% (22% for the year 2000/2001). Therefore if the income is retained by the trust and is not paid to, or expended on a beneficiary, it will bear tax at the rate of 34%. However if it is paid out to a beneficiary (or on his behalf) the trustees can give him a **tax credit voucher** of 34%. He or his representative can then claim back from the Revenue the difference between his top rate of tax (if under 34%) and the rate paid by the trust. For that reason if the trust **income** is used to pay residential care fees for the beneficiary the transfer of the money to the care home should be done in such a way as to leave no doubt that it has become part of his income, or is being expended on his behalf. (The trust deed must provide for the possibility both of direct payments to the beneficiary and indirect payments on his behalf so that the latter can be made in respect of his maintenance, etc.) Even if the income paid out by the trust is surplus to his requirements and is put in his savings account the difference in tax rates can still be reclaimed.

6.3 In the calculation of any income of the trust which is retained by the trust and which is not going to the beneficiary in the tax year in which it is earned, relief is given for expenses which are properly deductible from income such as accountancy fees, or some forms of interest. (Capital expenditure is not tax deductible even where the trust deed expressly provides that such expenditure should be paid out of the trust income. The general rule for distinguishing income from capital for this purpose is that " ...income must bear all outgoings of a recurrent nature, such as rates and taxes and interest on charges and incumbrances." - (Lord Templeman in *Carver v Duncan* (1985) STC 356)).

*contributed by a Member of the Chartered Institute of Taxation.

6.3.1 Example: *a discretionary trust has capital of £100,000 which produces income of £5,000 (gross) per annum.. Annual accountancy fees amount to £500. As this is a recurring expense it can be deducted from the gross income for the purposes of calculating the tax payable by the trustees. Therefore only £4500 will be taxable at 34% producing a tax bill of £1530. If however all the income is paid out to, or for, a beneficiary whose top rate of tax is 23%, the individual will receive £2970 with a tax credit voucher of £1530. He will then be able to reclaim 11%:-*

Gross Income paid by trust to beneficiary	4500
Less tax at 34% paid by trust	1530
Net income received from trust by beneficiary	2970
Tax due by beneficiary at 23% on £4500	1035
Tax reclaimable by beneficiary (£1530 - £1035)	**£495**

Normally the repayment claim will be made after the end of the relevant tax year. However if required, an interim claim can be made part way through the year, which could be useful if cash flow is a problem. The Revenue will expect the interim claim to include reasonable estimates of the expected income from all sources for the year. If they are satisfied they will pay out 75% of the amount claimed with the remaining 25% being repaid after the end of the tax year.

6.3.2 The beneficiary can in due course, if he wants, donate the tax rebate back to the trust (and thereby keep his retained capital below the £10,000 limit which is excluded from a local authority care fees assessment). This is a capital addition to the trust and has no income or capital tax gains consequences for either the individual or the trust provided a reasonable time elapses between the transfers. It could however be relevant if inheritance tax is an issue (see **6.9** regarding "additions").

6.3.3 Tip:- soon after a trust is set up income may be less important than it will be later when the settlor goes into care and the question of the trust contributing to a higher standard of accommodation arises. In the early years therefore it may be advisable to invest in low income high growth stocks or tax exempt investments such as National Savings Certificates to keep the income tax liability as low as possible.

6.3.4 Warning:- from 6 April 1999 individuals cannot reclaim the tax credits on **dividends.** If they were to receive payments from a discretionary trust, whose income was derived from dividends, and then reclaimed all or part of the 34% trust tax credit, they would effectively be reclaiming tax on dividends. In addition, dividends receivable by a trust are taxable at a new trust rate of 25% accounted for by the 10% tax credit and 15% paid by the trust, although when the dividend income is paid out to the beneficiaries it still carries a 34% tax credit. New trusts which have not built up a tax pool will require to account for the additional tax out of capital, or the income available to pay out to the beneficiaries will have to be reduced to cover the extra tax bill:-

Example:- if dividend income of £100 plus a tax credit of £11 was received by a discretionary trust in 1999/2000 and distributed to beneficiaries, the tax position would be as follows:-

Tax on trust income (£100 plus £11) @ 25%	27.75
Less dividend tax credit (10% of £111)	11.00
Tax payable by the trust (15% of £111)	16.75
Net income of the trust is £100 less £16.75	**83.25**
Distribution to beneficiaries (the cash dividend)	100.00
Less tax at 34% (tax credit)	34.00
Net payment to the beneficiaries	**66.00**
Further tax to be accounted for by the trustees	
(£34 less £16.75)	17.25
	83.25

Non-taxpaying beneficiaries can reclaim the full 34% tax credit, and beneficiaries whose top tax rate is less than 34% can reclaim the difference.

6.3.5 Note: the above rules are complicated, but they do not apply where the trust income comes from non-dividend (i.e. unfranked) sources, such as savings accounts, corporate bonds, (or unit trusts investing in either of these), or portfolios which have at least 60% invested in unfranked securities. None of these are affected by the rules illustrated above. The trust income from these is simply taxed at 34%, and the beneficiary claims back the difference between that and his own tax rate. Instead of paying out the net cash dividend, as shown above (£100 less 34% = £66), the trustees can pay out the whole interest received from an unfranked source - if the income in the above example had come from unfranked sources the trustees would have paid out £111 less 34% = £73.26. In the context of protecting capital from inclusion in a local authority residential care fees assessment, while minimising administration, and at the same time maximising income with a view to making a voluntary contribution to the fees, high income unfranked securities may therefore be the better choice of investment, but remember that a sale of ordinary shares to reinvest in such investments could give rise to a capital tax liability.

Capital Gains Tax
6.4 The transactions of trusts are also subject to the **Capital Gains Tax**

rules, the rate of tax being the same as for income tax, i.e. 34%. The calculation of the gain is done in the same way as for individuals and relief is available for **indexation** (an allowance for inflation). **Capital losses** from other disposals up to 6 April 1998 can also be used. Thereafter taper relief replaces indexation. As the amount of taper relief given depends on the number of **full years** of ownership careful consideration needs to be given to the precise timing of the disposal to obtain full advantage of the relief. In addition trusts have an annual capital gains **exemption** equal to one half of that available to individuals. For the year ending 5th April 2000 the individual's exempt amount is £7100 which means that a trust's exempt amount will be £3550. This exempt amount may be reduced further if more than one trust has been created by the settlor so that there is no advantage in creating a series of trusts.

6.5 Where transfer of the family home to a trust is the main concern the incidence of capital gains tax at the time of the transfer has to be considered. The gain which arises is the difference between the value of the property at the time of the transfer and the original cost adjusted for indexation and any capital expenditure since purchase. If the property was held at 31 March 1982 the value at that date can be substituted for the cost if advantageous, subject to the appropriate election being made. The gain on the property will however qualify for the principal private residence exemption and normally no capital gains tax will be payable by the individual. Any subsequent growth in value will be a gain in the hands of the trust but thanks to the decision in *Sanson and Another v Peay* ChD 1976 STC 494 the principal private residence exemption will still apply if the original owner has continued in occupation even if that occupation has only been at the discretion of the trustees. Even if for some reason the occupancy arrangements did not qualify for this exemption the tax liability would not be great as the following example shows:

6.5.1 *Example:- in 1991 **X** sets up a discretionary trust and gifts his house worth £95,000 to the trust. He bought the property in 1982 for £75,000, but there is no capital gains tax liability because the gain between 1982 and 1991 is covered by the principal private residence exemption. In 1997 **X** moves into a residential care home and the trustees obtain a price for the house net of expenses, of £105,000. If the gain between 1991 and 1997 was subject to capital gains tax, relief would first have to be given for the effect of inflation (indexation) over the five year period:-*

Proceeds from sale (after expenses, such as solicitor's fees, advertising etc)	105000
"Cost" to the trust (i.e. value when transferred to the trust by **X**)	95000
Apparent gain	10000
Less Allowance for inflation (indexation) say 4% of £95,000	3800

Chargeable gain	6200
Less annual exemption	3550
Taxable gain	2650

Capital gains tax payable would be £2650 @ 34%: £901

6.5.2 **Note**: if there are other assets within the trust such as shares a review should be undertaken as any losses on these can be offset against any chargeable gain on the house.

6.5.3 **Tip**: if a very large gain is realised the trustees may wish to consider reinvesting in a Venture Capital Trust. If the amount of the gain on the sale of the property is used to buy shares in a Venture Capital Trust no capital gains tax will be payable at the time the asset is sold. Instead the gain is rolled over into the shares. On a subsequent sale of the shares the capital gains tax may be collected but the gain could again be rolled over. The downside of Venture Capital Trusts of course is that they may be too risky an investment for the type of trust under consideration.

6.6 It will be obvious therefore that the incidence of capital gains tax if any is likely to be very small compared to the possible loss of the whole property if it is retained in the potential resident's personal ownership and taken into account in a residential care fees assessment.

Inheritance Tax

6.7 The question of liability for **Inheritance Tax** will arise only where the assets of an individual or a trust exceed **£231,000** in capital value which is the nil rate band for the year ending 5th April 2000. Capital value in excess of that amount is taxable at the rate of 40% on the death of an individual.

6.8 Inheritance Tax has also to be considered when making gifts or transfers of assets during one's lifetime. Transfers of value of less than £3000 are ignored but amounts in excess of £3000 are "potentially" exempt transfers and will escape Inheritance Tax if the donor survives for seven years from the date of the transfer. On death the value of the deceased's estate plus gifts or transfers within the previous seven years are taken into account and if the total exceeds the nil rate band in force at the time (currently £231,000), some Inheritance Tax may be payable. Transfers into a discretionary trust are chargeable lifetime transfers. Inheritance tax is payable at the rate of 20% of the value of the transfer but only if the donor has used up the nil rate band with previous transfers.

6.8.1 **Example:-** in 1997 **X** transfers his house worth £150,000 to a discretionary trust. He has already transferred in 1994 shares worth £120,000 to another discretionary trust set up for his son. Inheritance tax payable on the transfer to his own discretionary trust is calculated as follows :-

Value of transfer	150000
Balance of nil rate band:-	111000
(£231,000 less £120,000 being the amount of the earlier gift in 1994 to the son's trust)	
Amount chargeable	39000

IHT is payable on £39,000 at 20% and amounts to: **£7800**

If however **X** had made no transfers prior to setting up his own discretionary trust, the nil rate band would cover the whole value transferred to his own trust and no IHT would be payable.

6.9 Special charging provisions exist for discretionary trusts. While the tax legislation may appear complicated it should be remembered that the nil rate band of £231,000 still applies. Rates of tax thereafter are low and if the capital remains within the trust the charge will apply only every ten years - see section 64 of the Inheritance Tax Act 1984. The maximum rate which can apply is 6% of the value of the assets over £231,000 on the day before the **tenth anniversary** of the trust's creation. Account is also taken of the level of chargeable transfers by the settlor in the seven years prior to the trust being created. Therefore if the value of the settlor's gifts or transfers has not exceeded the nil rate band at the time he set up the trust the level of chargeable transfers at that time will be zero and as a result tax will be payable only on any amount by which the value of the assets exceeds £231,000 on the day prior to the anniversary as the nil rate band must be applied before the ten year charge is calculated. The nil rate band which will apply is the one in force at the time of the ten year charge. Assuming the current nil Rate band is not reduced in years to come, if the value of the trust at the ten year anniversary is still less than £231,000 no ten year charge will be payable.

Additions to settlements can create problems if the amounts added exceed the annual exempt amount of £3,000. This is because the chargeable transfer of value which is added will increase the settled capital of the trust. A comparison is then made between the settlor's chargeable transfers prior to commencement of the trust and the chargeable transfers prior to the addition, and the larger total is then used for the purposes of calculating ten year charges.

6.10 There are other occasions when a liability to inheritance tax can arise. The following are examples:

    i. Property ceases to be comprised in a settlement, for example when it is appointed out of the trust to a beneficiary.

    ii. The property ceases to be "relevant property", for example when it

Render Unto Caesar

remains within the trust but no longer at the trustees' discretion which can happen when an "interest in possession" is created. (The trustees still retain ownership of the asset until the trust deed dictates otherwise but any income arising from the asset belongs automatically to the beneficiary.)

     iii. The trustees reduce the value of the property within the trust by transferring the value elsewhere. This can cover deliberately not exercising a right - see section 65(9) of the Inheritance Tax Act 1984.

6.11 In all such cases however the **nil rate band** still applies and the incidence of inheritance tax can always be ignored if the estate itself or the total of transfers at the relevant time does not exceed £231,000 in value. If it does exceed that figure to calculate the level of the charge at times other than the ten year anniversary, the full ten year charge is reduced by the number of quarters in which the property has been in the discretionary trust, and where the ten year charge has not yet arisen a notional ten year period is created.

6.12 This outline of the incidence of taxation does make some generalisations for the sake of brevity, but it should demonstrate that while the incidence of taxation must be taken into account it need not be prohibitive to the setting up of a discretionary trust for the protection of the family's wealth, and if professional advice is sought at the outset many of the problems which could arise will be avoided.

Summary of time limits and escape routes

If there has been a carefully managed and well timed disposal of assets along the lines set out in preceding chapters there should be no need to refer to any of the notes below. The earlier and more complete the disposal of assets is the less able the local authority will be to reclaim their value or take them into account. The best destination for the assets in these circumstances will usually be a discretionary trust but no-one can forecast what the courts may decide or what changes governments may make in the law. It is to be hoped however that no government will be so bold as to depart from precedent and make such changes retrospective, nor would one expect any court or government to deny to the relatively less well-off the advantages of a discretionary trust for protection of assets against a care fees assessment when for centuries such advantages have been available to the very rich to protect their property both from the taxman, and the possible depredations of dissolute heirs and successors.

1. Where less than **six months** have elapsed since the donation of assets, or their transfer at an undervalue:

    (i) try to prove transfer of assets was done **not** "knowingly and with the intention of avoiding charges" - a very difficult task given the close juxtaposition of the date of gifting and the entry to care, and particularly difficult where circumstances point to residential care being in contemplation at the date of the asset transfer. See **2.19** and **2.20** (and in **Scotland** note the possible bankruptcy exception: **5.8**).

    (ii) postpone entry to Part III/Part IV accommodation (i.e. accommodation provided, or whose provision is arranged, by the local authority) until six months have passed and use assets to finance totally private care in a home, or at home, in the meantime but if an avoidance intention is alleged and cannot be disproved the local authority will apply **regulation 25** of the **1992 regulations** and treat the transferred assets as notional capital for assessment purposes (**see 3.1** and **3.2**).

    (iii) die, or be so ill as to require hospital, as opposed to nursing, care.

2. Where between **six months and two years** have elapsed since the donation of assets:

    (i) in **England and Wales** stave off the operation of section **341(2)** of the **Insolvency Act 1986** by prolonging the argument as long as possible and if need be by making some payments based on the local authority's assessment

Summary of Time Limits and Escape Routes

of notional capital; or move out of Part III accommodation and finance totally private care for the appropriate period.

(ii) in **Scotland** demonstrate that the donor did not become insolvent by the act of donation. See **5.6** and **5.9**.

3. Where between **two years and five years** have elapsed since the donation of assets:

   (i) in **England and Wales** demonstrate that the donor did not become insolvent by the act of donation, **and** that there was no intention of prejudicing the interests of possible future creditors. See **5.4**.

   (ii) in **Scotland** demonstrate that the donor did not become insolvent by the act of donation. See **5.6**.

4. Where more than **five years** have elapsed since the donation of assets:

   (i) in **England and Wales** ensure there is no evidence to suggest there was at the date of donation an intention to prejudice the interests of possible future creditors. See **5 .7** and **5.10**.

   (ii) in **Scotland** if faced by an unlikely challenge under the still extant common law of bankruptcy demonstrate that the donor did not become insolvent by the act of donation. See **5.6** and **5.9**.

5. In all cases if all else fails:

   (i) if already in care check that the accommodation really is "Part III/Part IV" accommodation, See **3.3** to **3.7** or

   (ii) make legal history by arguing that the disposal of assets was not a gift at all but payment for care or other services rendered by the donee (**4.22.1**, and **5.11** to **5.13**).

And remember in all cases, to avoid falling foul of the notional capital rules, be able to demonstrate that with regard to any donation or transfer at an undervalue *at any time* **there was no significant intention of avoiding payment of care fees.**

Draft Style of Discretionary Trust Deed

Part I of this draft contains the nomination of trustees, and hands over to the trustees an initial nominal sum of money.

Part II provides for them to receive the rest of the estate later, and from time to time (but the sooner all the estate passes to the trust the better), and contains the essential discretionary elements so that no one can insist on the settlor/truster exercising any purported right to obtain funds for his residential care from what was formerly his personal estate; and it also nominates a sufficiently wide class of beneficiaries who may benefit from exercise of the trustees' discretion right from the day the deed is signed thus reinforcing the intention that this deed is both irrevocable and an *inter vivos* trust deed disposing of property now and not a testamentary trust deed postponing disposal till the date of death.

Part III expands on what the trustees may do and provides some further standard guidance on what is to be done in certain circumstances (e.g. what to do with the funds when the settlor/truster dies).

Part IV contains some of the standard powers which lawyers always put into trust deeds; in the authors' opinion the first paragraph of this Part states in general terms all the business and administrative powers the trustees really need but convention dictates that some of the less obvious ones be specifically mentioned. It is not necessary to state, for example, as some drafts do, that the trustees shall have "power to sign cheques" as their having hands and brains and the power to use them is surely implicit in their choice, appointment, and acceptance of office; nor is there any mention in this style of a power to extract minerals or to harvest timbers: these may occasionally be necessary but are entirely inappropriate if the estate consists, for example, of an inner city flat and a savings account. Finally there is a specific declaration of irrevocability.

AB's Discretionary Trust

PART I I, **AB**, residing at ………………considering that I wish to make better provision for the management of my estate and for the after mentioned beneficiaries, namely me, the said **AB**, and my children, **BB** residing at ……………, **CB** residing at………………, and **DB** residing at………………… and their respective issue (all hereinafter referred to as the "beneficiaries") do hereby**:**

NOMINATE AND APPOINT as my trustees, (hereinafter referred to as the "trustees") for the purposes aftermentioned, myself the said **AB**, my son the said **BB**, my daughters, the said **CB** and the said **DB**, and **X**, solicitor, carrying on business at……………, and such other persons as may hereafter be appointed or assumed, and the acceptor or acceptors, survivor, or survivors of them as such trustees; of which any two trustees shall constitute a quorum at any meeting of trustees for the transaction of the business of my trust;

CONVEY and make over to, and in favour of, the said trustees the sum of Five Pounds sterling;

Draft Style of Discretionary Trust Deed

Part II **DIRECT AND APPOINT** that the said sum and any property, funds, and assets, of any kind in which my estate may from time to time, and at any time, be invested, together with any further or other property, funds, or assets, which may be conveyed or made over to the trustees by me or any other party, and any income accumulated thereon, (hereinafter referred to as "the trust estate") shall be held and applied by the trustees for the following purposes while I remain alive:-

First: To pay the expenses incurred in the execution and administration of the trust hereby created;

Second: To pay, apply, allocate, or appoint, to, or for the benefit of, the beneficiaries, the whole or any part of the trust estate whether it be the free income, or the capital, or any combination of them, and any accumulation of income (all of which are hereinafter referred to as the "trust funds"); any or all of which the trustees may do in exercise of the absolute discretion hereby conferred on them: **(i)** for the benefit of such one or more of the beneficiaries exclusive of the other, or others of them, as the trustees may decide; **(ii)** in such shares and proportions and in such a manner and subject to such provisions, limitations, conditions, and qualifications as the trustees may think fit; **(iii)** with, and subject to, the discretionary powers contained herein, all which discretionary powers may be exercised from time to time, and at any time, by the trustees, in whole or in part, as they at their sole discretion may decide; And the trustees may: **(i)** create interests in the possession, and the accumulation, and maintenance settlements; **(ii)** accumulate for such period during which income may lawfully be accumulated any income not so paid or applied or allocated and add it to capital;

Part III **AND I MAKE THE FOLLOWING DECLARATIONS: (One)** Without prejudice to the foregoing generality, the trustees may exercise the powers hereby conferred on them, to settle on such other trustees as the trustees may appoint or select for the purpose, the whole or part of the trust funds, to be held for any one or more of the beneficiaries; and this the trustees may do: **(i)** subject to such directions, authorities, powers, conditions, limitations, and restrictions, **(ii)** with such provisions for maintenance, education, support, advancement, and benefit, and **(iii)** subject to such other protective and other trusts exercisable at the discretion of the trustees or any other person or persons, as may seem appropriate to the trustees, and all interest created by such settlement in favour of any beneficiary shall become absolute and indefeasible;

(Two) The trustees' powers to accumulate income shall be exercisable only during the period of twenty one years from and after the date of this deed or during my lifetime, whichever is the shorter, and on the expiry of such period the trustees shall pay or apply the whole of the trust funds to, or for the benefit of, one or more of the beneficiaries;

(Three) All income provisions made by the trustees for a beneficiary shall be strictly alimentary, shall thereby not be assignable by the beneficiary, nor be affected by the beneficiary's debts, or anything the beneficiary may do, or by any arrestment or attachment which the beneficiary's creditors purport to impose;

Draft Style of Discretionary Trust Deed

(**Four**) If the trustees exercise their powers to confer on any of the beneficiaries rights of a continuing nature or to settle funds on them, they may do so expressly and irrevocably, or subject to such powers of cancellation or recall prior to the vesting date of such rights, as they, the trustees, may determine;
(**Five**) In the event of my death the trustees shall hold the trust funds for the benefit of my said children in the proportion of one-third for each, or in such proportion as they, the trustees, may determine; and may at their discretion pay over all or part of the trust funds to my children in the said proportion to each; and if any of my children predecease me the issue of such children shall take equally among them per stirpes the share which otherwise would have gone to the parent; and insofar as the trust funds are not disposed of in terms of the foregoing provisions they shall be made over to the estate of the last to die of my children and their issue absolutely, vesting taking place only when payment falls to be made.

Part IV **IN ADDITION AND WITHOUT PREJUDICE** to the powers, privileges and immunities enjoyed by trustees under statute or at common law, my trustees shall have the fullest powers to retain, realise, invest, purchase, lease or hire, and transfer property without realisation, and to manage the trust estate as if they were absolute beneficial owners; and they shall have power to do everything they may consider necessary or expedient for the administration of the trust; and, in particular and without prejudice to these general powers, my trustees shall have power:-
(**1**) To effect, maintain and acquire policies of insurance of whatever description; and to insure any property on whatever terms they think fit;
(**2**) To administer and manage any heritable or real property forming part of the trust estate; to repair, maintain, renew and improve said property and to erect additional buildings and structures; to grant, vary and terminate leases and rights of tenancy or occupancy over or in said property, all as my trustees may think proper and as if they were absolute beneficial owners of the trust estate;
(**3**) To continue or to commence any business, whether alone or in conjunction or in partnership with any other persons, or through any companies, for such periods as my trustees may think proper; to appoint or employ any trustee or any other person in any capacity in relation to such business and to pay suitable remuneration for services, including pension provisions for any employees or their dependents; and to delegate or entrust to any person the control and management of such business to such extent as my trustees may think fit; and my trustees (a) may employ for the purposes of such business such part of the income or capital of the trust estate as they think proper; (b) shall exercise only such control or supervision of such business as they shall think fit; (c) shall be entitled to be relieved from the trust estate from all personal responsibility for any loss arising from such business operations; and (d) shall be entitled to retain personally any remuneration for their services;
(**4**) To defend, pursue, or settle any court proceedings which they or others may raise in connection with the trust estate having taken appropriate professional advice; and to use the trust funds for settlement of any expenses or costs which may be awarded against them as trustees;
(**5**) To allow the estate or any part thereof to be registered in the names of, or held,

Draft Style of Discretionary Trust Deed

or the documents of title to be held, by any person, firm, corporation or other body as their nominee;

(6) To delegate any power or powers of making, managing, realising or otherwise dealing with any investment or deposit comprised in the trust estate to any person or persons upon such terms as to remuneration or otherwise as my trustees may think fit:

(7) To accept any other property which may be made over to them;

(8) To decide what is capital and what is income and the proportion on which expenses are to be charged against capital and income respectively;

(9) To set apart and appropriate specific property of any description to represent the whole or part of the share, prospective or otherwise, of any beneficiary at such valuation as my trustees shall determine so that thereafter the particular share or part shall have the full benefit and the whole risk of the appropriated investments or assets;

(10) To settle with any beneficiary entitled to any part of the trust estate by conveying to him or her in satisfaction of said entitlement, such specific property or money, as to my trustees shall seem proper and at such valuation as they shall determine; and to compel acceptance accordingly;

(11) To enter into any transaction or do any act otherwise authorised by law or by this Deed notwithstanding that any trustee is or might be thus acting as *auctor in rem suam* or in conflict of interest between such trustee and himself as an individual or as trustee of any other Trust or any partnership of which my trustee is a partner or any company of which my trustee is a shareholder or director or in relation to any combination of these capacities, provided that the trustee or trustees with whom there is, or may be, any such conflict is or are not the sole trustee or trustees;

(12) To participate in the exercise of any discretion granted to my trustees notwithstanding that a trustee is or may be a, or the sole, beneficiary in whose favour the discretion is then exercised provided that there is at least one trustee not so favoured;

(13) To appoint one or more of their own number to act as Solicitor or Agent in any other capacity and to allow him or them the same remuneration as to which he or they would have been entitled if not a trustee or trustees;

(14) To renounce for themselves or their successors in office the power to exercise any of the foregoing powers as if said powers were vested in them beneficially and not as trustees;

(15) And my trustees shall not be liable for depreciation in value of the property in the trust estate nor for omissions or errors in judgement, nor for neglect in management, nor for insolvency of debtors nor for the acts, omissions, neglects or defaults of each other or of any agent employed by them.

AND I DECLARE THAT this trust is irrevocable and is to be interpreted, administered according to, and governed by the Law of Scotland;

In Witness Whereof:

National Assistance Act 1948

THE LEGISLATION

The following pages contain, in chronological order, the primary and subordinate legislation, referred to in bold type in the text, updated to 31st January 2000, and emphasis added by the author.

NATIONAL ASSISTANCE ACT 1948

SECTION 21: Duty of local authorities to provide accommodation *(England and Wales, including amendments by the Community Care (Residential Accommodation) Act 1998)*

(1) Subject to and in accordance with the provisions of this Part of this Act, a local authority may with the approval of the Secretary of State, and to such extent as he may direct shall, **make arrangements for providing--(a) residential accommodation** for persons aged eighteen or over who by reason of age, illness, disability or any other circumstances are in need of care and attention **which is not otherwise available** to them;

(2A) In determining for the purposes of paragraph (a) or (....) of subsection (1) of this section whether care and attention are otherwise available to a person, a local authority shall disregard so much of the person's capital as does not exceed the capital limit for the purposes of section 22 of this Act.

(2B) For the purposes of subsection (2A) of this section—

(a) a person's capital shall be calculated in accordance with assessment regulations in the same way as if he were a person for whom accommodation is proposed to be provided as mentioned in subsection (3) of section 22 of this Act and whose ability to pay for the accommodation falls to be assessed for the purposes of that subsection; and

(b) "the capital limit for the purposes of section 22 of this Act" means the amount for the time being prescribed in assessment regulations as the amount which a resident's capital (calculated in accordance with such regulations) must not exceed if he is to be assessed as unable to pay for his accommodation at the standard rate; and in this subsection "assessment regulations" means regulations made for the purposes of section 22(5) of this Act.

SECTION 22: **Charges to be made for accommodation.**

(1) Subject to section 26 of this Act, where a person is provided with accommodation under this Part of this Act the **local authority providing the accommodation shall recover from him the amount of the payment which he is liable to make** in accordance with the following provisions of this section.

(2) Subject to the following provisions of this section, the payment which a person is liable to make for any such accommodation shall be in accordance with a **standard rate** fixed for that accommodation by the authority managing the premises in which it is provided and **that standard rate shall represent the full cost to the authority of providing that accommodation.**

(3) Where a person for whom accommodation in premises managed by any local authority is provided, or proposed to be provided, under this Part of this Act satisfies the local authority that he is unable to pay therefore at the standard rate, **the authority shall assess his ability to pay** .... and accordingly **determine at what lower rate** he shall be liable to pay for the accommodation.

(4) In assessing for the purposes of the last foregoing subsection a person's ability to pay a local authority shall assume that he will need for **his personal requirements such sum per week as may be prescribed by the Minister, or such other sum as in special circumstances the authority may consider appropriate.**

National Assistance Act 1948

SECTION 26: **Provision of accommodation in premises maintained by voluntary organisations.**
(1) ....

(2) Any arrangements made by virtue of . . . .. this section **shall** provide for **the making by the local authority to the other party thereto of payments in respect of the accommodation provided** at such rates as may be determined by or under the arrangements and subject to subsection (3A) below **the local authority shall recover from each person for whom accommodation is provided** under the arrangements the amount of the refund which he is liable to make in accordance with the following provisions of this section.

(3) Subject to subsection (3A) below a person for whom accommodation is provided under any such arrangements shall, in lieu of being liable to make payment therefore in accordance with section twenty-two of this Act, **refund to the local authority any payments made in respect of him** under the last foregoing subsection: **Provided that** where a person for whom accommodation is provided, or proposed to be provided, under any such arrangements satisfies the local authority that he is unable to make a refund at the **full rate** determined under that subsection, subsections (3) to (5) of section twenty-two of this Act shall, with the necessary modifications, apply as they apply where a person satisfies the local authority of his **inability to pay at the standard rate** as mentioned in the said subsection (3).

(3A) Where accommodation in any premises is provided for any person under arrangements made by virtue of this section and the **local authority, the person concerned and the voluntary organisation or other person managing the premises** (in this subsection referred to as "the provider") agree that this subsection shall apply--

(a) so long as **the person concerned makes the payments for which he is liable** under paragraph (b) below, he shall **not be liable to make any refund** under subsection (3) above and the **local authority shall not be liable to make any payment** under subsection (2) above in respect of the accommodation provided for him;

(b) **the person concerned shall be liable to pay to the provider** such sums as would otherwise (under subsection (3) above) be liable to pay by way of refund to the local authority; and

(c) **the local authority shall be liable to pay to the provider the difference** between the sums paid by virtue of paragraph (b) above and the payments which, but for paragraph (a) above, the authority would be liable to pay under subsection (2) above.

SECTION 42: **Liability to maintain wife or husband, and children.**
(1)(a) **a man shall be liable to maintain his wife** and his children, and
(b) **a woman shall be liable to maintain her husband** and her children.

SECTION 43: **Recovery of cost of assistance from persons liable for maintenance.**
(1) Where assistance is given or applied for by reference to the requirements of any person (in this section referred to as a person assisted), . . . the local authority concerned may make a complaint to the court against any **other person** who for the purposes of this Act is **liable to maintain the person assisted.**

(2) On a complaint under this section **the court** shall have regard to all the circumstances and in particular to the resources of the defendant, and may order the defendant to pay such sum, weekly or otherwise, as **the court may consider appropriate.**

(3) For the purposes of the application of the last foregoing subsection to payments in respect of assistance given before the complaint was made, a person **shall not be treated as having at the time when the complaint is heard any greater resources than he had at the time when the assistance was given.**

(4) In this section the expression "assistance" means . . . the provision of accommodation under Part III of this Act (hereinafter referred to as "assistance under Part III of this Act"); and the

expression "the court" means a court of summary jurisdiction appointed for the commission area (within the meaning of the Justices of the Peace Act 1979) where the assistance was given or applied for.

SOCIAL WORK (SCOTLAND) ACT 1968

SECTION 12: General social welfare duties of local authorities *(including amendments by the Community Care (Residential Accommodation) Act 1998).*

(1) It shall be the duty of every local authority to promote social welfare by making available advice, guidance and assistance on such a scale as may be **appropriate** for their area, and in that behalf to make arrangements and to provide or secure the provision of such facilities **(including the provision or arranging for the provision of residential and other establishments)** as they may consider **suitable** and **adequate**, ...

(3A) In determining for the purposes of this section whether to provide assistance by way of residential accommodation to a person, a local authority **shall** disregard so much of the person's capital as does not exceed the capital limit for the purposes of **section 22** of the **National Assistance Act 1948**.

(3B) For the purposes of subsection (3A) of this section—

(a) a person's capital shall be calculated in accordance with assessment regulations in the same way as if he were a person for whom accommodation is proposed to be provided under this Act and whose ability to pay falls to be assessed for the purposes of section 22(3) of the National Assistance Act 1948; and

(b) "the capital limit for the purposes of section 22 of the National Assistance Act 1948" means the amount for the time being prescribed in assessment regulations as the amount which a resident's capital (calculated in accordance with such regulations) must not exceed if he is to be assessed as unable to pay for his accommodation at the standard rate; and in this subsection "assessment regulations" means regulations made for the purposes of section 22(5) of the National Assistance Act 1948 or section 87(5) of this Act.

SECTION 12A: Duty of local authority to assess needs.

(1) Subject to the provisions of this section, where it appears to a local authority that any person for whom they are under a duty or have a power to provide, or to secure the provision of, community care services may be in need of any such services, the authority—

(a) shall make an **assessment of the needs** of that person for those services; and

(b) having regard to the results of that assessment, shall then decide- whether the needs of that person call for the provision of any such service.

SECTION 14: Home help and laundry facilities.

(1) It shall be the duty of every local authority to provide on such scale as is adequate for the needs of their area, or to arrange for the provision on such a scale as is so adequate of, **domiciliary services** for households where such services are required owing to the presence, or the proposed presence, of a person in need ...., and every such authority shall have power to provide or arrange for the provision of laundry facilities for households for which domiciliary services are being, or can be, provided under this subsection.

SECTION 59: Provision of residential and other establishments.

(1) ...., it shall be the duty of a local authority to provide and maintain such residential and other establishments as may be required for their functions under this Act, or arrange for the provision of such establishments.

(2) For the purpose of discharging their duty under the foregoing subsection a local authority may -

(a) **themselves provide** such establishments as aforesaid; or
(b) join with another local authority in providing such establishments as aforesaid: or
(c) **secure the provision of** such establishments by voluntary organisations or other persons persons including other local authorities.

SECTION 87: **Charges that may be made for services and accommodation.**

(1) Subject .... to the following provisions of this section, a local authority providing a service under this Act .... **may recover such charge (if any) for it as they consider reasonable.**

(lA) If a person—
(a) avails himself of a service provided under this Act............; and
(b) satisfies the authority providing the service that his **means are insufficient** for it to be reasonably practicable for him to pay for the service the amount which he would otherwise be obliged to pay for it, the authority shall not require him to pay **more** for it than it appears to them that it is **reasonably practicable** for him to pay.

(2) Persons,.......... for whom accommodation is provided under this Act..........., **shall be required to pay for that accommodation** in accordance with the subsequent provisions of this section.

(3) Subject to the following provisions of this section, accommodation provided under this Act..........shall be regarded as **accommodation provided under Part III** of the National Assistance Act 1948, and sections 22(2) to (8) and 26(2) to (4) (as amended by the Schedule to the Housing (Homeless Persons) Act 1977, paragraph 2(1) of Schedule 4 to the Social Security Act 1980, section 20 of the Health and Social Services and Social Security Adjudications Act 1983 and paragraph 32 of Schedule 10 to the Social Security Act 1986) (charges for accommodation and provision of accommodation in premises maintained by voluntary organisations) and sections 42 (as amended by paragraph 5 of Schedule 1 to the Law Reform (Parent and Child) (Scotland) Act 1986) and 43 of the said Act of 1948 **(which make provision for the mutual maintenance of wives and husbands** and the maintenance of their children **by recovery of assistance from persons liable for maintenance and for affiliation orders, etc.)** shall apply accordingly.

(4) In the application of the said section 22, for any reference to the Minister there shall be substituted a reference to the Secretary of State, and in the application of the said section 26, any references to **arrangements** under a scheme for the provision of accommodation shall be construed as references to arrangements made by a local authority with a voluntary organisation or any other person or body for the provision of accommodation under this Act............

HEALTH AND SOCIAL SERVICES AND SOCIAL SECURITY ADJUDICATIONS ACT 1983

SECTION 17: **Charges for local authority services in England and Wales.**

(1) Subject to subsection (3) below, an authority providing a service to which this section applies may recover such **charge** (if any) for it as they consider **reasonable.**

(2) This section applies to services provided under the following enactments--
(a) section 29 of the National Assistance Act 1948 **(welfare arrangements for blind, deaf, dumb and crippled persons etc);**
(b) section 45(1) of the Health Services and Public Health Act 1968 **(welfare of old people);** (c) Schedule 8 to the National Health Service Act 1977 **(care of mothers and young children, prevention of illness and care and after-care and home help and laundry facilities);**
(d) section 8 of the Residential Homes Act 1980 **(meals and recreation for old people);** and (e) paragraph 1 of Part II of Schedule 9 to this Act other than the provision of services for which payment may be required under section 22 or 26 of the National Assistance Act 1948.

Health and Social Services and S S Adjudications Act 1983

(3) If a person --
(a) avails himself of a service to which this section applies, and
(b) satisfies the authority providing the service that **his means are insufficient** for it to be **reasonably practicable** for him to pay for the service the amount which he would otherwise be obliged to pay for it, the authority shall not require him to pay more for it than it appears to them that it is **reasonably practicable** for him to pay.

SECTION 21: **Recovery of sums due to local authority where persons in residential accommodation have disposed of assets.**

(1) Subject to the following provisions of this section, where -
(a) a person avails himself of Part III accommodation; and
(b) that person **knowingly and with the intention of avoiding** charges for the accommodation-
  (i) **has transferred** any asset to which this section applies to some other person or persons **not more than six months** before the date on which he begins to reside in such accommodation; or
  (ii) transfers any such asset to some other person or persons while residing in the accommodation; **and**
(c) either -
  (i) the **consideration** for the transfer is **less than the value of the asse**t; or
  (ii) there is **no consideration** for the transfer, **the person or persons to whom the asset is transferred** by the person availing himself of the accommodation **shall be liable to pay to the local authority** providing the accommodation or arranging for its provision **the difference** between the amount assessed as due to be paid for the accommodation by the person availing himself of it and the amount which the local authority receive from him for it.

(2) This section applies to **cash and any other asset** which falls to be taken into account for the purpose of assessing under section 22 of the National Assistance Act 1948 the ability to pay for the accommodation of the person availing himself of it.

(4) Where a person has transferred an asset to which this section applies to **more than one person**, the liability of each of the persons to whom it was transferred shall be **in proportion** to the benefit accruing to him from the transfer.

(5) A person's liability under this section shall **not exceed the benefit accruing to him** from the trade.

(6) Subject to subsection (7) below, the **value** of any asset to which this section applies, other than cash, which has been transferred shall be taken to be the amount of the consideration which would have been realised for it if it had been sold on the **open market by a willing seller** at the time of the transfer.

(7) For the purpose of calculating the value of an asset under subsection (6) above there shall be **deducted** from the amount of the consideration--(a) the amount of any **incumbrance on the asset**; and (b) a reasonable amount in respect of the **expenses of the sale**.

(8) In this Part of this Act **"Part III accommodation"** means accommodation provided under sections 21 to 26 of the National Assistance Act 1948, and, in the application of this Part of this Act to Scotland, means accommodation provided under the Social Work (Scotland) Act 1968 or ....

SECTION 22: **Arrears of contributions charged on interest in land in England and Wales.**

(1)................where a person who avails himself of Part III accommodation provided by a local authority in England, Wales or Scotland-
(a) **fails to pay** any sum assessed as due to be paid by him for the accommodation; and
(b) **has a beneficial interest in land** in England or Wales, the **local authority may**

create a charge in their favour on his interest in the land.

(2) In the case of a person who has interests in more than one parcel of land the charge under this section shall be upon his interest in such one of the parcels as the local authority may determine.

(4) Subject to subsection (5) below, a charge under this section shall be in respect of any amount assessed as due to be paid which is outstanding from time to time.

(7) A charge under this section shall be created by a declaration in writing made by the local authority.

SECTION 23: **Arrears of contributions secured over interest in land in Scotland.**

(1)......... where a person (hereinafter referred to as the debtor) who avails himself of Part III accommodation provided by a local authority in Scotland, England or Wales-

(a) **fails to pay** any sum (hereinafter referred to as the debt) assessed as due to be paid by him for the accommodation; and

(b) **has an interest in land** in Scotland (as defined in section 9(8) of the Conveyancing and Feudal Reform (Scotland) Act 1970), the local authority may make in their favour .... an order (hereinafter referred to as a **charging order**) over that interest in land **in respect of the amount of the debt.**

SECTION 24: **Interest on sums charged or secured over interest in land.**

(1) Any sum charged on or secured over an interest in land ..... shall **bear interest** from the day after that on which the person for whom the local authority provided the accommodation **dies.**

ENDURING POWERS OF ATTORNEY ACT 1985
(England and Wales)

SECTION 1: **Enduring power of Attorney to survive mental incapacity of donor.**

(1) Where an individual creates a power of attorney which is an **enduring power** within the meaning of this Act then-

(a) the power shall **not be revoked by any subsequent mental incapacity** of his; but

(b) upon such incapacity supervening the donee of the power may not do anything under the authority of the power except as provided by subsection (2) below or as directed or authorised by the court under section 5 unless or, as the case may be, until the instrument creating the power is registered by the court under section 6; and

(c) section 5 of the Powers of Attorney Act 1971 (protection of donee and third persons) so far as applicable shall apply if and so long as paragraph (b) above operates to suspend the donee's authority to act under the power as if the power had been revoked by the donor's mental incapacity.

(2) Notwithstanding subsection (l)(b) above, where the attorney has made an application for registration of the instrument then, until the application has been initially determined, the attorney may take action under the power—

(a) to maintain the donor or prevent loss to his estate; or

(b) to maintain himself or other persons in so far as section 3(4) permits him to do so.

(3) Where the attorney purports to act as provided by subsection (2) above then, in favour of a person who deals with him without knowledge that the attorney is acting otherwise than in accordance with paragraph (a) or (b) of that subsection, the transaction between them shall be as valid as if the attorney were acting in accordance with paragraph (a) or (b).

BANKRUPTCY (SCOTLAND) ACT 1985

SECTION 34: Gratuitous alienations.

(1) Where this subsection applies, an alienation by a debtor shall be **challengeable**
....
(2) ....where.....................(c) the alienation took place on a **relevant day**.

(3) For the purposes of paragraph (c) of subsection (2) above, the day on which an alienation took place shall be the day on which the alienation became completely effectual; and in that paragraph **"relevant day"** means, if the alienation has the effect of favouring—

(a) a person who is an associate of the debtor, a day not earlier than **5 years** before the date of sequestration, the granting of the trust deed or the debtor's death, as the case may be; or

(b) any other person, a day not earlier than **2 years** before the said date.

(4) On a challenge being brought under subsection (1) above, the court shall grant decree of reduction or for such restoration of property to the debtor's estate or other redress as may be appropriate, but the court shall **not grant such a decree if the person seeking to uphold the alienation** establishes—

(a) that immediately, or at any other time, after the alienation the **debtor's assets were greater than his liabilities**; or

(b) that the alienation was made for adequate consideration; or

(c) that the alienation—(i) was a birthday, Christmas or other conventional gift; or (ii) was a gift made, for a charitable purpose, to a person who is not an associate of the debtor, which having regard to all the circumstances, it was reasonable for the debtor to make: Provided that this subsection shall be without prejudice to any right or interest acquired in good faith and for value from or through the transferee in the alienation.

SECTION 36: Unfair preferences.

(1) Subject to subsection (2) below, subsection (4) below applies to a transaction entered into by a debtor, whether before or after the coming into force of this section, which has the effect of **creating a preference in favour of a creditor** to the prejudice of the general body of creditors, being a preference created not earlier than **6 months** before— (a) the date of sequestration of the debtor's estate (if, in the case of a natural person, a date within his lifetime); ....

(2) Subsection (4) below shall not apply to any of the following transactions—

(a) a transaction in the ordinary course of trade or business;

(b) a payment in cash for a debt which when it was paid had become payable unless the transaction was collusive with the purpose of prejudicing the general body of creditors;

(c) a transaction whereby the parties thereto undertake reciprocal obligations (whether the performance by the parties of their respective obligations occurs at the same time or at different times) unless the transaction was collusive as aforesaid; ....

(3) For the purposes of subsection (1) above, the day on which a preference was created shall be the day on which the preference became completely effectual.

(4) A transaction to which this subsection applies shall be challengeable by—(a) any creditor who is a creditor by virtue of a debt incurred on or before the date of sequestration, ...

(5) On a challenge being brought under subsection (4) above, the court, if satisfied that the transaction challenged is a transaction to which this section applies, shall grant decree of reduction or for such restoration of property to the debtor's estate or other redress as may be appropriate: Provided that this subsection shall be without prejudice to any right or interest acquired in good faith and for value from or through the creditor in whose favour the preference was created.

INSOLVENCY ACT 1986
(England and Wales)

SECTION 341: "Relevant time".

(1) Subject as follows, the time at which an individual enters into a transaction at an undervalue or gives a preference is a **relevant time** if the transaction is entered into or the preference given--

(a) in the case of a transaction at an undervalue, at a time in the period of **5 years** ending with the day of the presentation of the bankruptcy petition on which the individual is adjudged bankrupt,

(b) in the case of a preference which is not a transaction at an undervalue and is given to a person who is an associate of the individual (otherwise than by reason only of being his employee), at a time in the period of **2 years** ending with that day, and

(c) in any other case of a preference which is not a transaction at an undervalue, at a time in the period of **6 months** ending with that day.

(2) Where an individual enters into a transaction at an undervalue or gives a preference at a time mentioned in paragraph (a), (b) or (c) of subsection (1) (not being, in the case of a transaction at an undervalue, a time less than 2 years before the end of the period mentioned in paragraph (a)), that time is **not a relevant time** for the purposes of sections 339 and 340 unless the individual

(a) is **insolvent** at that time, or

(b) **becomes insolvent** in consequence of the transaction or preference; but the requirements of this subsection are presumed to be satisfied, **unless the contrary is shown,** in relation to any transaction at an undervalue which is entered into by an individual with a person who is an associate of his (otherwise than by reason only of being his employee).

(3) For the purposes of subsection (2), an individual is **insolvent** if (a) he is **unable to pay his debts as they fall due,** or (b) the value of his assets is less than the amount of his liabilities, taking into account his contingent and **prospective liabilities.**

SECTION 423: **Transactions defrauding creditors.**

(1) This section relates to transactions entered into at an undervalue; and a person enters into such a transaction with another person if -

(a) he makes a gift to the other person or he otherwise enters into a transaction with the other on terms that provide for him to receive no consideration;

(b) he enters into a transaction with the other in consideration of marriage; or

(c) he enters into a transaction with the other for a consideration the value of which, in money or money's worth, is significantly less than the value, in money or money's worth, of the consideration provided by himself.

(2) Where a person has entered into such a transaction, the court may, if satisfied under the next subsection, make such order as it thinks fit for -

(a) restoring the position to what it would have been if the transaction had not been entered into, and

(b) protecting the interests of persons who are victims of the transaction.

(3) In the case of a person entering into such a transaction, an order shall only be made if the **court is satisfied** that it was entered into by him for the purpose—

(a) of **putting assets beyond the reach of a person who is making, or may at some time make,** a claim against him, or

(b) of otherwise prejudicing the interests of such a person in relation to the claim which he **is making or may make.**

SECTION 424: **Those who may apply for an order under s.423.**

(1) An application for an order under section 423 shall not be made in relation to a transaction except—

(a) in a case where the debtor has been adjudged bankrupt or is a body corporate which is being wound up or in relation to which an administration order is in force, by the official receiver, by the trustee of the bankrupt's estate or the liquidator or administrator of the body corporate or (with, the leave of the court) by a victim of the transaction;

(b) in a case where a victim of the transaction is bound by a voluntary arrangement approved under Part I or Part VIII of this Act, by the supervisor of the voluntary arrangement or by any person who (whether or not so bound) is such a victim; or (c) in any other case, **by a victim of the transaction.**

NATIONAL HEALTH SERVICE AND COMMUNITY CARE ACT 1990

SECTION 47: **Assessment of needs for community care services.** *(England and Wales)*

(1) Subject to subsections (5) and (6) below, where it appears to a local authority that any person for whom they may provide or arrange for the provision of community care services may be in need of any such services, the authority--

(a) shall carry out an **assessment of his needs** for those services; and

(b) **having regard to the results of that assessment** shall then decide whether his needs call for the provision by them of any such services.

LAW REFORM (MISCELLANEOUS PROVISIONS) (SCOTLAND) ACT 1990

SECTION 71: **Powers of attorney.**

(1) Any rule of law by which a factory and commission or power of attorney **ceases to have effect in the event of the mental incapacity of the granter shall not apply to** a factory and commission or **power of attorney granted on or after the date on which this section comes into force.**

SOCIAL SECURITY (ATTENDANCE ALLOWANCE) REGULATIONS 1991 (SI 1991 NO 2740) *(as amended)*

REGULATION 7: **Persons in certain accommodation other than hospitals.**

(1) Except in the cases specified in paragraphs (2) and (3) and subject to regulations 7A and 8, a person **shall not be paid** any amount in respect of an **attendance allowance** for any period where throughout that period he is a person for whom accommodation is provided--

(a) in pursuance of-- (i) Part III of the National Assistance Act 1948 . . . , or (ii) Part IV of the Social Work (Scotland) Act 1968 or section 7 of the Mental Health (Scotland) Act 1984;

(b) in circumstances where the cost of the accommodation is borne wholly or partly out of public or local funds in pursuance of those enactments or of any other enactment relating to persons under disability ... . . ; or

(c) in circumstances where the cost of the accommodation **may be** borne wholly or partly out of public or local funds in pursuance of those enactments or of any other enactment relating to persons under disability . . .

REGULATION 8: **Exemption from regulations 6 and 7.**

(6) Regulation 7 **shall not apply,** except in a case to which **paragraph (7) applies,** in any particular case for any period during which--

(a) the person for whom the accommodation is provided-- **(i)** is not entitled to **income support**; **(ii)** is not entitled to **housing benefit**; or **(iii)** is not a member of a married or unmarried couple for whom an amount is included for income support purposes in the weekly applicable amount of the other member; and

(b) the **whole of the cost of the accommodation** is met-- **(i)** out of his **own resources**, or partly out of his own resources and partly with assistance from another person or a charity; **(ii)** on his behalf by another person or a charity.

(7) This paragraph **applies** in the case of a person who is residing in a home **owned or managed, or owned and managed, by a local authority.**

NATIONAL ASSISTANCE
(ASSESSMENT OF RESOURCES) REGULATIONS 1992
(SI 1992 NO 2977)

REGULATION 2: **Interpretation** *(as amended by The National Assistance Assessment of Resources) (Amendment No 2) Regulations 1998.*

(1) "**occupational pension**" means any pension or other periodical payment under an occupational pension scheme but does not include any discretionary payment out of a fund established for relieving hardship in particular cases;

"**prospective resident**" means a person for whom accommodation is proposed to be provided under Part III of the Act;

"**resident**" means a pErson who is provided with accommodation under Part III of the Act or is a prospective resident;

(4) In these Regulations, unless the context otherwise requires, any reference to a resident's accommodation, or to accommodation provided for a resident, shall be construed in the case of a resident who is a prospective resident as a reference to accommodation which is proposed to be provided for him under Part III of the Act.

REGULATION 16: **Capital treated as income.**

(4) Any payment of **capital** made or due to be made to a local authority by a third party pursuant to an agreement between the local authority and the third party in connection with the liability of the resident to pay the local authority for his accommodation shall be treated as part of the **income** of the resident, unless it is a **voluntary** payment made for the purpose of **discharging any arrears** of payments required by the local authority from the resident for his accommodation.

REGULATION 17: **Notional income.**

(1) A resident shall be treated as possessing income of which he has deprived himself for the purpose of decreasing the amount that he may be liable to pay for his accommodation.

(2) Subject to paragraph (3), a resident shall be **treated as possessing** any income which would be treated as income possessed by a claimant of income support under paragraphs (2) to (4) of regulation 42(4) of the Income Support Regulations **(notional income).** *[Income Support (General) Regulations 1987, SI No 1967].*

(4) Subject to paragraph (5), a resident shall be treated as possessing any income **paid or due to be paid** to a local authority **by a third party** pursuant to an agreement between the local authority and the third party made in connection with the liability of the resident to pay the local authority for his accommodation.

(5) A resident shall not be treated as possessing any **voluntary** payment of income **made by a third party** to a local authority for the purpose of discharging any arrears of the payments required by the local authority from the resident for his accommodation.

National Assistance (Assessment of Resources) Regulations 1992

REGULATION 20: **Capital Limit.**

No resident shall be assessed **as unable to pay** for his accommodation at the standard rate if his capital calculated in accordance with regulation 21 **exceeds £16,000.**

REGULATION 21: **Calculation of Capital.**

(1) The capital of a resident to be taken into account shall, subject to paragraph (2), be the whole of his capital calculated in accordance with this Part and any income treated as capital ....

(2) There shall be **disregarded** from the calculation of a resident's capital under paragraph (1) any capital, where applicable, specified in Schedule 4.

REGULATION 22: **Income Treated as Capital.**

(4) Except any income derived from capital disregarded under paragraph 1, 2, 5, 10 or 16 of Schedule 4, any **income** of a resident which is derived from capital shall be treated as **capital** but only from the date on which it is normally due to be paid to him.

....

(6) Any payment which would be treated as capital under paragraph (8) of regulation 4 of the Income Support Regulations(b) **(income treated as capital)** shall be treated as capital.

REGULATION 25: **Notional capital** *(as amended by The National Assistance Assessment of Resources) (Amendment) Regulations 1998..*

(1) A resident may be treated as possessing actual capital of which he has deprived himself for the purpose of decreasing the amount that he may be liable to pay for his accommodation except - **(a)** where that capital is derived from a payment made in consequence of any personal injury and is placed on trust for the benefit of the resident; or **(b)** to the extent that the capital which he is treated as possessing is **reduced** in accordance with **regulation 26,** or **(c)** any sum to which paragaph 44(a) or 45(a) of Schedule 10 to the Income Support Regulatons **(disregard of compensaton for personal injuries which is administered by the Court) refers.**

(2) Subject to paragraph (3), a resident may be **treated as possessing** any payment of capital which would be treated as capital possessed by a claimant of income support under paragraph (2) or (3) of regulation 51 of the Income Support Regulations (notional capital).

(3) For the purposes of paragraph (2) - **(a)** regulation 51(2)(c) of the Income Support Regulations shall apply as if for the reference to Schedule 10 to those Regulations there were substituted a reference to **Schedule 4 to these Regulations**; and **(b)** regulation 51(3)(a)(ii) of the Income Support Regulations shall apply as if for the words from 'the food, ordinary" to the end of sub-paragraph (a)(ii) there were substituted the words "any item which was taken into account when the standard rate was fixed for the accommodation provided".

....

(5) Where a resident is **treated as possessing capital** under paragraph (1) or (2), the foregoing provisions of this Part shall apply for the purposes of calculating its amount **as if it were actual capital** which he does possess.

REGULATION 26: **Diminishing notional capital rule.**

(1) Where a resident is treated as possessing capital under regulation 25(1) (for the purposes of this regulation called **"reducible notional capital"**), for each week or part of a week that a local authority has determined that the resident shall be liable to pay for his accommodation at a higher rate than that at which he would have been assessed as liable to pay if he had no reducible notional capital, the amount of his reducible notional capital shall be **reduced** by the method prescribed in paragraph (2).

(2) The local authority shall **reduce** the amount of the resident's reducible notional

National Assistance (Assessment of Resources) Regulations 1992

capital by the **difference** between (a) the **higher rate** referred to in paragraph (1); and (b) **the rate which he would have been assessed as liable to pay** for his accommodation for that week or part of a week if he had been assessed as possessing no reducible notional capital.

REGULATION 27: Capital jointly held.

(1) Where a resident and one or more other persons are beneficially entitled in possession to **any capital asset except any interest in land** - (a) they shall be treated as if each of them were entitled in possession to an equal share of the whole beneficial interest in that asset; and (b) that asset shall be treated as if it were actual capital.

(2) Where a resident and one or more other persons are beneficially entitled in possession to **any interest in land-** (a) the resident's share shall be valued at an amount equal to the price which his interest in possession would realise if it were sold to a **willing buyer**, less 10 per cent and the amount of any incumbrance secured solely on his share of the whole beneficial interest; and (b) the value of his interest so calculated shall be treated as if it were actual capital.

REGULATION 28: Calculation of tariff income from capital.

(1) Where a resident's capital calculated in accordance with this Part **exceeds £10,000** it shall be treated as equivalent to a weekly income of £1 for each complete £250 in excess of £10,000 but not exceeding £16.000.

SCHEDULE 2: Sums to be disregarded in the calculation of earnings.

1. In the case of a resident who-- **(a)** has been employed as an employed earner; or **(b)** had the employment been in Great Britain, would have been so employed, and whose employment has been terminated or is interrupted, any earnings paid or due to be paid in respect of that employment.

2. In the case of a resident--**(a)** who has been engaged in any work as a self-employed earner; or **(b)** had the work been in Great Britain, would have been so engaged, and who has ceased to be so engaged, from the date of cessation of his work any earnings derived from that work except earnings to which regulation 12(2) or (3) **(royalties etc.)** applies.

3. (1) In a case to which this paragraph applies, the amount specified in paragraph 4(1) of Schedule 8 to the Income Support Regulations **(disregard for claimants in receipt of a disability premium etc.)**.(2) This paragraph applies where a resident--**(a)** receives an invalid care allowance or receives income support which includes an amount by way of a carer premium or a disability premium under Schedule 2 to the Income Support Regulations **(applicable amounts)**; or **(b)** is under the age of 60 and--**(i)** receives an attendance allowance, a disability living allowance, a disability working allowance, a mobility supplement, an invalidity pension, . . . or a severe disablement allowance, or **(ii)** is provided with an invalid carriage or other vehicle under section 5(2)(a) of the National Health Service Act 1977 **(invalid carriages)** or under section 46 of the National Health Service (Scotland) Act 1978 **(provision of vehicles)**, or **(iii)** receives any payment by way of a grant under paragraph 2 of Schedule 2 to the National Health Service Act 1977 **(additional provisions as to vehicles)** or under section 46 of the National Health Service (Scotland) Act 1978 **(provision of vehicles)**, or **(iv)** is registered as blind under section 29(4)(g) of the Act **(welfare arrangements for blind persons etc.)**, or, in Scotland, is registered as blind in a register maintained by or on behalf of a regional or islands council, or **(v)** for a continuous period of not less than 28 weeks has provided medical evidence of incapacity in support of a claim for sickness benefit, invalidity pension or severe disablement allowance, or **(vi)** would be in receipt of attendance allowance or the care component of disability living allowance had it not been withdrawn solely because he has been in accommodation provided under Part III of the Act for more than 4 weeks; or **(c)** has attained the age of 60 and--**(i)** satisfies one of the conditions set out in heads (i) to (vi) in paragraph (b), **(ii)** satisfied one of those conditions before he attained the

age of 60, and **(iii)** is in remunerative work and has continued to be engaged in remunerative work since before he attained the age of 60; or **(d)** is not one of a couple and has a child living with him.

4. In a case to which paragraph 3 does not apply to the resident, the amount specified in paragraph 9 of Schedule 8 to the Income Support Regulations **(disregard for those not qualifying for the higher disregard).**

5. Any earnings which would be disregarded under paragraph 11 of Schedule 8 to the Income Support Regulations **(earnings outside the United Kingdom).**

6. Any amount which would be disregarded under paragraph 4 of Schedule 9 to the Income Support Regulations **(part of statutory sick pay).**

SCHEDULE 3, Part I: Sums to be Disregarded.

1. Any amount paid by way of tax on income which is taken into account under regulation 15 **(calculation of income other than earnings).**

2. Any payment in respect of any expenses incurred by a resident who is--**(a)** engaged by a **charitable or voluntary** body; or **(b)** a **volunteer**, if he otherwise derives no remuneration or profit from the employment.

3. Any payment which would be disregarded under paragraph 3, 4A or 5 of Schedule 9 to the Income Support Regulations **(employed earner expenses, statutory sick pay in Northern Ireland and housing benefit).**

4. The **mobility component** of any disability living allowance.

5. Any payment which would be disregarded under paragraph 8 of Schedule 9 to the Income Support Regulations.

6. If the resident is a **temporary** resident--**(a)** any **attendance allowance;** or **(b)** the **care component** of any disability living allowance.

7. Any **concessionary payment** made to compensate for the non-payment of-- **(a)** any payment specified in paragraph 4 or 6; or **(b)** any income support.

8. Any amount which would be disregarded under paragraph 10 or 11 of Schedule 9 to the Income Support Regulations **(payments to medal recipients and educational awards).**

9. Any amount which would be disregarded under paragraph 13 or 14 of Schedule 9 to the Income Support Regulations **(participants in training schemes and job start allowance).**

10.(1) Except where sub-paragraph (2) applies, and subject to Paragraphs 29 and 31, the amount specified in paragraph 15(1) of Schedule 9 to the Income Support Regulations **(charitable or voluntary payments)** of any charitable payment or of any voluntary payment made or due to be made at regular intervals other than any payment which is to be disregarded under paragraph 24.

(2) Subject to paragraph 29, any charitable payment or voluntary payment made or due to be made at regular intervals which is intended and used for any item which was not taken into account when the standard rate was fixed for the accommodation provided.

10A.(1) ....,where a resident- **(a)** is **not residing with his spouse,** and **(b)** at least **50 per cent of any occupational pension** of his , or of **any income** from a **personal pension scheme** or a **retirement annuity contract** of his is being paid to, or in in respect of, his spouse for that spouse's maintenance, an amount equal to 50 per cent of the pension, pensions or income concerned; (2)......(3).......

11. Any amount which would be disregarded under paragraph 16 of Schedule 9 to the Income Support Regulations **(specified pensions),** but as if the reference in paragraph 16 of Schedule 9 to the Income Support Regulations to paragraphs 36 and 37 of Schedule 9 to the Income Support Regulations were a reference to paragraph 31 of this Schedule and as if the reference in paragraph 16(a) of Schedule 9 to the Income Support Regulations to paragraphs 8 or 9 of Schedule 9 to the Income Support Regulations were a reference to paragraphs 5 or 6 of this Schedule.

National Assistance (Assessment of Resources) Regulations 1992

12. Any payment which would be disregarded under paragraphs 17 to 20 of Schedule 9 to the Income Support Regulations **(annuities, payments by third parties towards living costs, contractual payments in respect of occupation of a dwelling and payments by lodgers).**

13. Any income **in kind.**

14. (1) Any income derived from capital to which the resident is or is treated under regulation 27 **(capital jointly held)** as beneficially entitled but, subject to sub-paragraph (2), not income derived from capital disregarded under paragraph 1, 2, 5, 10 or 16 of Schedule 4. **(2)** Any income derived from capital disregarded under paragraph 2, 16 or 18 of Schedule 4 but only to the extent of any mortgage repayments and payments of council tax or water charges which the resident is liable to make in respect of the dwelling or premises in the period during which that income accrued.

15. Any income which would be disregarded under paragraph 23 of Schedule 9 to the Income Support Regulations **(income outside the United Kingdom).**

16. Any amount which would be disregarded under paragraph 24 of Schedule 9 to the Income Support Regulations **(charge or commission for converting income into sterling).**

17. Any payment made to a resident in respect of a child or young person who is a member of his family--**(a)** in accordance with regulations made pursuant to section 57A of the Adoption Act 1976 **(permitted allowances)**; **(b)** in accordance with a scheme approved by the Secretary of State under section 57(4) of the Adoption Act 1976 **(approved schemes)** or section 51 of the Adoption (Scotland) Act 1978 **(schemes for payment of allowances to adopters)**; **(c)** which is a payment made by a local authority in pursuance of section 1 (1) of, and paragraph 15 of Schedule 1 to, the Children Act 1989 **(local authority contribution to a child's maintenance where a child is living with a person as a result of a residence order)**; **(d)** which is a payment by a local authority towards the cost of the accommodation and maintenance of a child following a custodianship order under section 33 of the Children Act 1975; or **(e)** which is a payment made by a local authority in pursuance of section 50 of the Children Act 1975 **(payments towards maintenance of children).**

18. Any payment which would be disregarded under paragraph 26 or 28 of Schedule 9 to the Income Support Regulations **(provision of accommodation and maintenance for children in care, and local authorities' duty to promote the welfare of children and powers to grant financial assistance to persons in or formerly in their care).**

19. Any payment received under an **insurance policy, taken out to insure against the risk of being unable to maintain repayments on a loan to acquire or retain an interest in a dwelling occupied as the home,** or for repairs and improvements to the dwelling, and used to meet such repayments, to the extent that it does not exceed the aggregate of--**(a)** the amount payable, calculated on a weekly basis, of any interest on the loan; **(b)** the amount of any payment, calculated on a weekly basis, due on the loan attributable to the repayment of capital; and **(c)** the amount, calculated on a weekly basis, of the premium due on that policy.

20. Any payment which would be disregarded under Paragraph 31 of Schedule 9 to the Income Support Regulations **(social fund payments).**

21. Any payment of income which under regulation 22 **(income treated as capital)** is to be treated as capital.

22. Any payment which would be disregarded under paragraph 33 of Schedule 9 to the Income Support Regulations **(pensioner's Christmas bonus).**

23. Any payment which would be disregarded under paragraph 38 of Schedule 9 to the Income Support Regulations **(resettlement benefit).**

24. Any payment which would be disregarded under paragraph 39 of Schedule 9 to the Income Support Regulations **(the Fund, the Macfarlane Trusts and the Independent Living Fund).**

25. Any amount which would be disregarded under paragraphs 40 to 51 of Schedule 9 to the Income Support Regulations (**housing benefit compensation, supplementary benefit compensation, housing benefit supplement compensation, juror and witness payments, community charge rebate, community charge benefit reduction of liability for personal community charge, special war widows payments, travelling expenses and health service supplies, welfare food payments, prison visiting scheme payments, and disabled persons' employment payments**).

26. Any payment of income support made towards housing costs determined in accordance with Schedule 3 to the Income Support Regulations (**housing costs**).

27. Any **housing costs of any temporary resident**, including any fuel charges ..... included in the rent of a dwelling to which he intends to return, to the extent that the local authority consider it reasonable in the circumstances to do so.

28. Any **council tax benefit**.

28A. Any **child benefit**, except in circumstances where a resident is accompanied by the child in respect of whom the child benefit is payable and accommodation is provided for that child under Part III of the Act.

28B. Any payment which would be disregarded under paragraph 53 of Schedule 9 to the Income Support Regulations.

28C. Any payment which would be disregarded under paragraphs 54 to 56 of Schedule 9 to the Income Support Regulations.

SCHEDULE 3, Part II: **Special Provisions Relating to Charitable or Voluntary Payments and Certain Pensions.**

29. Paragraph 10 shall not apply to any payment which is made or due to be made--(**a**) by a person for the maintenance of any member of his family or of his former partner or of his children; or (**b**) by a third party pursuant to an agreement between the local authority and that third party in connection with the liability of the resident to pay the local authority for his accommodation.

30. For the purposes of paragraph 10(1), where a number of charitable or voluntary payments fall to be taken into account in any one week they shall be treated as though they were one such payment.

31. The total income to be disregarded pursuant to paragraphs 10(1) and 11 shall in no case exceed the amount per week specified in paragraph 36 of Schedule 9 to the Income Support Regulations (**ceiling for aggregated disregards**).

SCHEDULE 4: **Capital to be Disregarded** *(as amended by The National Assistance (Assessment of Resources) (Amendment) Regulations 1998 (1998 No. 497) and The National Assistance (Assessment of Resources) (Amendment No 2) Regulations 1998 (1998 No. 1730)*

1(1) In the case of a **temporary resident** who is not a prospective resident, the value of one dwelling (and not more than one dwelling) from which he is absent in circumstances where--

(**a**) he is taking reasonable steps to dispose of the dwelling in order that he may acquire another dwelling which he intends to occupy as his home; or (**b**) he intends to return to occupy that dwelling as his home and the dwelling to which he intends to return is still available to him.

(2) In the case of a temporary resident who is a prospective resident,

the value of one dwelling (and not more than one dwelling) in circumstances where he intends, on being provided in fact with accommodation under that Part of the Act—

(a) to take reasonable steps to dispose of the dwelling in order that he may acquire another dwelling which he intends to occupy as his home; or (b) to return to occupy that dwelling as his home; and the dwelling to which he intends to return is available to him;

2(l) Subject to sub-paragraph (2), the value of any premises which would be disregarded

National Assistance (Assessment of Resources) Regulations 1992

under paragraph 2 or 4 of Schedule 10 to the Income Support Regulations **(premises acquired for occupation, and premises occupied by a partner, a former partner or a relative)**. *[The paragraph 4 disregard in the Income Support (General) Regulations 1987 (SI No 1967) as amended, reads as follows: "Any premises occupied in whole or in part by (a)..... (b) the former partner of a claimant.....as his home; but this provision shall not apply where the former partner is a person from whom the claimant is **estranged or divorced**."]*

(2) For the purposes of sub-paragraph (1), paragraph 4 of Schedule 10 to the Income Support Regulations shall apply as if for the words "that person is aged 60 or over or is incapacitated" there were substituted the words "that partner or relative is aged 60 or over, is incapacitated or is a child whom the resident is liable to maintain by virtue of section 42(1) of the National Assistance Act 1948 **(liability to maintain wife or husband and children)**.

3. The value of the proceeds of sale of any premises which would be disregarded under paragraph 3 of Schedule 10 to the Income Support Regulations **(proceeds of sale from premises formerly occupied)**.

4. Any future interest in property which would be disregarded under paragraph 5 of Schedule 10 to the Income Support Regulations **(future interests in property other than in certain land or premises)**.

5. Any assets which would be disregarded under paragraph 6 of Schedule 10 to the Income Support Regulations **(business assets)**, but as if in sub-paragraph (2) of that paragraph for the words from "the claim for income support" to the end of that sub-paragraph there were substituted (a) in the case of a resident other than a prospective resident the words "the accommodation was initially provided"; (b) in the case of a prospective resident, the words " the local authority began to assess his ability to pay for his accommodation under these regulations".

6. Any amount which would be disregarded under paragraph 7 of Schedule 10 to the Income Support Regulations **(arrears of specified payments)**, but as if the reference in sub-paragraph (a) of that paragraph to paragraph 6, 8, 9 or 9A of Schedule 9 to the Income Support Regulations **(other income to be disregarded)** were a reference to paragraphs 4 to 6 of Schedule 3 to these Regulations.

7. Any amount which would be disregarded under paragraph 8 or 9 of Schedule 10 to the Income Support Regulations **(property repairs and amounts deposited with a housing association)**.

8. Any **personal possessions** except those which had or have been acquired by a resident with the intention of reducing his capital in order to satisfy a local authority that he was unable to pay for his accommodation at the standard rate or to reduce the rate at which he would otherwise be liable to pay for his accommodation.

9. Any amount which would be disregarded under paragraph 11 of Schedule 10 to the Income Support Regulations **(income under an annuity)**.

10. Any amount which would be disregarded under paragraph 12 of Schedule 10 to the Income Support Regulations **(personal injury trusts)**.

11. Any amount which would be disregarded under paragraph 13 of Schedule 10 to the Income Support Regulations **(a life interest or a liferent)**. *[The paragraph 13 disregard in the Income Support (General) Regulations 1987 (SI No 1967) as amended, reads as follows: "The value of the **right to receive** any income under a life interest or from a liferent."]*

12. The value of the right to receive any income which is disregarded under paragraph 5 of Schedule 2 or paragraph 15 of Schedule 3 **(earnings or other income to be disregarded)**.

13. Any amount which would be disregarded under paragraphs 15, 16, 18 or 19 of Schedule 10 to the Income Support Regulations **(surrender value of life insurance policy, outstanding installments, social fund payments and tax refunds on certain loan interest)**.

14. Any capital which under regulation 16 or 39 **(capital treated as income and student loans)** is to be treated as income.

The National Assistance (Sums For Personal Requirements) Regulations 1999

15. Any amount which would be disregarded under paragraphs 21 to 24 of Schedule 10 to the Income Support Regulations **(charge or commission for converting capital into sterling, the Macfarlane Trusts, the Fund and the Independent Living Fund, personal or occupational pensions, and rent).**

16. The value of any premises which would be disregarded under paragraph 27 or 28 of Schedule 10 to the Income Support Regulations **(premises a claimant intends to occupy).**

17. Any amount which would be disregarded under paragraphs 29 to 43 of Schedule 10 to the Income Support Regulations **(fund payments in kind, training bonuses, housing benefit compensation, supplementary benefit compensation, housing benefit supplement compensation, juror or witness payments, community charge rebate, reduction of liability for personal community charge, housing grants, travelling expenses and health service supplies, welfare food payments, prison visiting scheme payments, special war widows payments, disabled persons' employment payments, and blind homeworkers' payments).**

18. The value of any premises occupied in whole or in part by a **third party** where the local authority consider it would be **reasonable** to disregard the value of those premises.

19. Any amount which would be disregarded under paragraph 44(a) or 45(a) of Schedule 10 to the Income Support Regulations **(compensation for personal injuries which is administered by the Court).**

THE NATIONAL ASSISTANCE
(SUMS FOR PERSONAL REQUIREMENTS)
REGULATIONS 1999
(SI 1999 No 549)

REGULATION 2: **Sums needed for personal requirements.**

2. The sum which under **section 22(4)** of the **National Assistance Act 1948** a local authority **shall** assume that a person will need for his **personal requirements** shall be £14.75 per week.

Yule v South Lanarkshire Council (No 2)

This was the second hearing in the *Yule* judicial review, heard by the same single judge in the Outer House of the Court of Session. It remains unreported, and legal aid has been granted for an appeal to the Inner House against the judgment which was issued on 12th May 1999. The decision of the appeal court should be available by the summer of 2000. The lower court upheld the local authority's decision that Mrs Yule had given her house to her granddaughter in order to avoid its inclusion in an assessment of means for residential care, and that its value should be included in the assessment as notional capital (regulation 25 of the 1992 Regulations).

> No evidence was put before the court other than the exchange of correspondence between Mrs Yule's solicitors and the local authority. Counsel for the local authority submitted there had been sufficient material before the local authority to enable them to decide that Mrs Yule's purpose was to decrease the amount which she might be liable to pay. In making this decision, it was further submitted, the local authority did not require to hold it "proved" that Mrs Yule was seeking to deprive herself of assets in order to decrease her liability. The decision was administrative, not judicial. The official making the decision had no power to require the production of information, but had to proceed on the basis of such information as was available. In that situation there was no requirement for the official to hold facts proved before he could make a decision. Cases relating to other forms of means tested benefit (which counsel for Mrs Yule had prayed in aid) were of no assistance because the provisions relating to those benefits (unlike the residential care provisions) incorporated an appeal procedure.

> The Court decided that the question before it was whether the decision of the local authority was so unreasonable that no reasonable authority could ever have come to it, or more particularly, was there material before the local authority on which the decision could reasonably have been reached. Approaching the case on this basis the Court took the following facts in to account:
>
> 1 Mrs Yule was 78 when she disponed the fee of her dwelling house to her granddaughter, and at the same time executed a power of attorney in favour of her son;
>
> 2 She retained the liferent of the house and continued to live in it until her accident;
>
> 3 She could have achieved the same practical result by making a will in

favour of her granddaughter - no clear explanation was offered why Mrs Yule chose to give the house to the granddaughter by *inter vivos* transfer rather than by will;

4 There was a conflict between information given by Mrs Yule's son to social workers carrying out a community care assessment in May 1996 to the effect that her health had been deteriorating for six or seven years, and a later letter from the solicitors claiming that the lady's health had been excellent as at March 1995.

The following is an extract from the judgment:-

"The respondents were entitled to draw inferences from the information received by them. The power of attorney indicated that the petitioner's affairs required to be managed by others. It is reasonable to draw from that the inference that the petitioner's health was not perfect at the time of execution. It is a fact of life, which the respondents were entitled to take into account, that persons in their late seventies are increasingly likely to require nursing home accommodation. The avoidance of the requirement to meet the full cost of nursing home accommodation provided a motive for making the gift by *inter vivos* transfer of the property rather than by will. In so far as any other motive or explanation was provided to the respondents, they were entitled to reject it. In my view no satisfactory motive or explanation was in fact proffered. The provision of conflicting information as to the petitioner's health provided a justification for drawing an adverse inference from information which was capable of affording such an inference.

"The decision on matters of fact is left to the respondents and there is no appeal. Accordingly the weight given by the respondents to particular pieces of evidence is entirely a matter for them and not open to challenge. I do not accept the petitioner's submission that the respondents could only make the decision which they did if there was evidence that the claimant knew of the existence of a capital limit, and that she had foreseen the making of an application for the relevant benefit. In seeking to operate Regulation 25 local authorities are unlikely to be met with ready admission that the purpose of a transfer of a capital asset of an elderly person was to decrease the amount that he or she might be likely to pay for accommodation provided under the 1968 Act [**Social Work (Scotland) Act 1968**]. There will be cases in which the elderly person is incapable of forming any intention to transfer or of understanding the nature and purpose of any arrangement. In such cases he or she may be assisted by relatives or advisers. There is no power to compel the provision of information, and the local authority must determine the purpose of the transfer from the information which has been provided to it. In such circumstances the true purpose of any transfer may be ascertained or inferred without any specific finding as to the state of knowledge or intention of the elderly person."

Fortunately these ominous (and not entirely logical) pronouncements will be tested in the appeal court, and if need be, the House of Lords. The suggestion that an elderly person who becomes frail enough to require care will automatically make arrangements for avoiding full liability for its cost and that any arrangements he makes will be motivated by an avoidance intention may be a shrewd one, but it is also a gross insult, to which injury is added by the assertion that the local authority is entitled to reject any other motive or explanation which is offered without a quasi-judicial examination of the facts. When coupled with counsel's submission (which was not specifically rejected by the Court) that the local authority's decision is administrative rather than judicial, and that it can be made without findings in fact, the judgment seeks to impose a most unfair regime in which a decision of fundamental importance to the elderly person and his relatives could be made with little or no regard to the facts by the party (the local authority) who will benefit most from a decision in that party's favour. It would also be very unfortunate if elderly persons were to be saddled with an intention to avoid liability for care fees just because, in acknowledgement of frailty already upon them, or in humble expectation of what the future may hold, they execute a power of attorney (or transfer their assets to a discretionary trust). Indeed many will do so not with a view to a future entry to care, but rather with an intention of avoiding such a fate by ensuring that the burden of administering their material affairs is alleviated, and that they are not tempted into unwise investments (thus, incidentally, maintaining such ability as they may have to pay for any care which does become necessary in the future).

The appeal court can be expected to test the lower court's decision against the definition of the scope and purpose of judicial review provided by Lord Clyde in *Reid v Secretary of State for Scotland* (H.L.(Sc.)) [1999]2 WLR 28 at page 54: 'Judicial review involves a challenge to the legal validity of the decision. It does not allow the court of review to examine the evidence with a view to forming its own view about the substantial merits of the case. It may be that the tribunal whose decision is being challenged has done something which it had no lawful authority to do. It may have abused or misused the authority which it had. It may have departed from the procedures which either by statute or at common law as a matter of fairness it ought to have observed. As regards the decision itself it may be found to be perverse, or irrational, or grossly disproportionate to what was required. Or the decision may be found to be erroneous in respect of a legal deficiency, as for example, through the absence of evidence, or of sufficient evidence, to support it. or through account being taken of irrelevant matter, or through a failure for any reason to take account of a relevant matter, or through some misconstruction of the terms of the statutory provision which the decision-maker is required to apply. But while the evidence may have to be explored in order to see if the decision is vitiated by such legal deficiencies it is perfectly clear that in a case of review, as distinct from an ordinary appeal, the court may not set about forming its own preferred view of the evidence."

Whatever the outcome of the appeal, it should be remembered that Yule considered only notional capital and the proper conduct of assessments under **regulation 25** of the **1992 Regulations**. Inclusion of notional capital in an assessment increases only what is due to be paid by the resident in care. If there are no assets out of which the debt can be satisfied a ruling on notional capital will have no practical disadvantage for the resident nor provide any benefit for the local authority. Yule says nothing about the proper interpretation of **section 21** of the **Health and Social Services and Social Security Adjudication Act 1983** with its more draconian provisions for reclaiming the value of assets transferred within six months prior to entry to care. And while it has in the past been generally anticipated that **section 21(1)(b)** - "knowingly and with the intention of avoiding" - should be interpreted in the same way as "for the purpose of" in **regulation 25**, if Yule is upheld on appeal, the difference between the two provisions could be argued to advantage.

Index

AB's Discretionary Trust	71	Delay Inadvisable	61
Actual Capital	13	Deprivation of Income	22
Arguing the Case	39	Deprivations	48
Assessment Procedures	9	Discretionary Trusts	27
Attendance Allowance	24	Disposals more than six months prior to entry to care	45
Avoid Insolvency Proceedings	57		
Bankruptcy (Scotland) Act 1985	81	Disposals within the six month period or after entry to care	43
Barclays Bank v Eustice	31		
Beware The Difference	11	**Dispose of the Assets**	24
"Boyd loophole"	25	Disregarded Income	21
Capital Assessment	12	Domiciliary Care	36
Capital Disregards	15	**Draft Style of Discretionary Trust Deed**	71
Capital Exhaustion	14	*Ellis v Chief Adjudication Officer*	27
Capital Gains Tax	64	Enduring Powers Of Attorney Act 1985	80
Capital Held On Trust	19	Health And Social Services And Social Security Adjudications Act 1983	78
Capital Jointly Held	17		
Carver v Duncan	62	Income Assessment	21
Choosing The Trustees	32	Income Recovery	22
Complaints Procedure	47	Income Tax	62
Controlling The Trustees	33	Inheritance Tax	66
Dangerous Disposals	26	Innocent Intention Essential	58
Dearth of Precedent	41	Insolvency Act 1986	82
Declarations	33	Intention	30
Defend a Deprivation	39	Irrevocability	29

Index

Know The Rules	9	Social Security Commissioners' Decisions:-	
Law Reform (Miscellaneous Provisions) (Scotland) 1990	83	CA/11185/95	25
Lawson v Coombes	21	CIS/24/1990	30
Midland Bank PLC v Wyatt	59	CIS/494/1990	50
National Assistance Act 1948	75	CIS/030/93(*82/94)	20
National Assistance (Assessment of Resources) Regulations 1992	84	CIS/242/1993	56,60
		CIS/7097/95	19
National Health Service and Community Care Act 1990	83	CSIS/453/95	35
		R(SB)38/85	53,56
Notional Capital	13	R(SB)40/85	52
Postpone the Day	34	R(SB) 9/91	54,56
Postponing Entry To Part III Accommodation	34	R(SB) 12/91	51
		Social Work (Scotland) Act 1968	77
Power of Attorney	33	Spousal Liability	22
"Pseudo Part III" Accommodation	35	*Steane v Chief Adjudication Officer and Another*	25
Purposes	31		
Quinn (for Harris deceased) and Others v Chief Adjudication Officer	35	**Summary of time limits and escape routes**	69
R v Sefton Metropolitan Borough Council	26	Tariff Income	14
R v Chief Constable for Warwickshire ex parte F.	46	*The Heritable Reversionery Company Ltd v Millar*	20
R v Gloucestershire CC, ex p Radar	12,48	**The Legislation**	75
R v Somerset County Council ex parte Harcombe	16	The National Assistance (Sums for Personal Requirements) Regulations 1999	91
R. v Islington London Borough Council ex parte Rixon	37	The Recompense Argument	60
		The Royal Commission on Funding of Long Term Care for the Elderly	7
Re Kumar (a bankrupt), ex parte Lewis v Kumar and Another	60	The Solvency Defence	57
R v Gloucestershire County Council and Another, ex parte Barry	38	The Way to Court	43
		Timing	29
Reid v Secretary of State for Scotland	46,94	*Upper Crathes Fishings Ltd v Baileys Executors*	18
Render Unto Caesar	62	*Yule v South Lanarkshire Council*	41,46
Self Financing	24	*Yule v South Lanarkshire Council (No 2)*	33,39,40,41,42,43,45,92
Social Security (Attendance Allowance) Regulations 1991	83		

Further copies of
Residential Care Fees: Defend The Assets!
can be ordered by telephone or fax,
if paid for by credit card (Visa or Access).
Telephone/fax number: 0131 664 3326.